The Teacher and Integration

by

Gertrude Noar

Student National Education Association

National Commission on Teacher Education and Professional Standards

National Education Association
1201 Sixteenth Street, Northwest,
Washington, D. C. 20036

ii

FOREWORD

This book was prepared in the belief that college graduates who become teachers this fall and in the years immediately ahead will make a substantial contribution to effective integration in our nation's schools. It is the first in a new series of Student NEA publications designed to provide college students and beginning teachers with useful information about important educational issues. The Student National Education Association is concerned with encouraging its membership—over 120,000 college students—to think through and act upon important social and educational issues. This first publication in the series is consistent with the ongoing interest and work of the Student NEA in human relations and the welfare of youth.

The National Commission on Teacher Education and Professional Standards (NCTEPS), the sponsoring commission for Student NEA, sees itself as an agency of change working to bring about constructive innovation in American education. The purposes of this book are directly related to major NCTEPS concerns—improving the education of teachers, before and after they begin to teach, and creating conditions in the schools which will encourage good teachers and good teaching.

We believe that most graduating seniors and beginning teachers are committed to the ideal of equal educational opportunity and experience. The school year 1966-67 offers an unusual opportunity for thousands of new teachers to make a real difference in the lives of children, whatever their color or background. We feel this challenge will be met with sensitivity and skill, making the late 1960's a time when college students going into teaching will apply their understanding and intelligence in meeting one of the most urgent educational and human challenges of our times.

We're putting our money on students and teachers who will see in the integration of schools a unique chance to apply their resources and concern for human dignity in working with the children of this country.

The process of school integration will not work if teachers, administrators, parents, and others stand aside and view it with detachment. School integration will work if people in and out of the school become intellectually and emotionally involved and committed to making it work. This book is designed to help teachers develop confidence that it can work.

This book was written also to counteract a good deal of misinformation which exists about minority group children and their education. Accurate information and practical suggestions are badly needed to assist teachers in their work in rapidly changing schools. This book is not presented as the final word but rather as a constructive approach to the day-by-day work of the teacher. The spirit in which it is written is one of confidence in the resources for human understanding of both teachers and children and in their ability to solve important problems.

We hope that many readers will be both reassured and encouraged as they read this book and as they undertake teaching assignments which are and will continue to be difficult, demanding, and often frustrating. We know that for some readers it will evoke strong feelings. We know, too, that these strong feelings can be the basis for constructive action and positive change. We urge the reader to share his reactions with fellow students and teachers. We hope that groups of college students and groups of teachers will use this book as a basis for continuing discussion about teaching and learning.

We are deeply indebted to the author, Miss Gertrude Noar. It has been a joy to come to know and share her commitment to the purposes and spirit of this book and to realize her dedication to the value of human dignity.

Dirck W. Brown
Associate Secretary, NCTEPS

Washington, D.C.
June 1966

iv

ACKNOWLEDGEMENTS

We wish to express our appreciation to the many people throughout the country—college students, teachers, administrators, supervisors, college and university faculty, staff persons, and others —who responded so helpfully to requests for assistance in reacting to the manuscript and to the ideas discussed in this book.

We are especially indebted to Mrs. Elizabeth Koontz, president of the NEA Department of Classroom Teachers; Mr. James Williams, NEA Southeast regional representative; Mrs. Toba G. Mayerson, of Philadelphia, Pennsylvania; members of the Ohio Association for Supervision and Curriculum Development; college students and faculties at The Ohio State University and Jackson (Mississippi) State College; and teachers, students, and administrators in Chattanooga, Tennessee, and other school systems who shared their work and ideas with the author. A special word of thanks goes to Miss Geraldine Pershing, NCTEPS production editor, for her imaginative and hard work, and to Miss Barbara Gladysiewicz, NCTEPS program assistant, for helping the author to develop the bibliographic material included.

We are indebted also to Dr. Robert Coles of Harvard University, Dr. Daniel C. Thompson of Dillard University, and Mrs. Theron Jacobson of Decatur, Illinois, for the use of their published material, and to their respective publishers—*Daedalus* and the American Academy of Arts and Sciences; the Bureau of Publications, Teachers College, Columbia University; and *Educational Leadership* and the Association for Supervision and Curriculum Development. Appreciation also goes to UNESCO for excerpts from *UNESCO Chronicle*.

Student NEA Executive Committee, 1965-66

Lane Hotchkiss, *President;* Ball State University, Muncie, Indiana

Vincent Matulaitis, Jr., *Vice-President;* State College at Worcester, Massachusetts

Judi Gustafson, *Secretary;* Glassboro State College, New Jersey

Jack Allen, *Associate Vice-President;* Montana State College, Bozeman

Wayne Bledsoe, *Associate Vice-President;* University of Arkansas, Fayetteville

Lynne M. Douglas, *Associate Vice-President;* New Mexico State University, University Park

Raymond N. Kuma, *Associate Vice-President;* Benedict College, Columbia, South Carolina

Rodney L. Nutting, *Associate Vice-President;* Northwest Nazarene College, Nampa, Idaho

National Commission on Teacher Education and Professional Standards, 1965-66

Warren G. Hill, *Chairman;* President, Trenton State College, New Jersey

Howard Lee Nostrand, *Vice-Chairman;* Professor of Romance Languages and Literature, University of Washington, Seattle

Clara E. Cockerille, Professor of Education, Westminster College, New Wilmington, Pennsylvania

George W. Denemark, Dean, School of Education, University of Wisconsin—Milwaukee

Frank L. Hildreth, Vice-Principal, North High School, Des Moines, Iowa

Sue Jarvis, Teacher, Nelson Elementary School, Kansas City, Missouri

Paul Kelley, Principal, South High School, Knoxville, Tennessee

Jean R. Moser, Coordinator of Special Studies and Programs, Baltimore County Schools, Towson, Maryland

J. B. Wooley, Dean, Southeastern Louisiana College, Hammond

Consultants

Lane Hotchkiss, President, Student NEA

Earl A. Johnson, Chairman, Organization of State TEPS Chairmen and Consultants

Rolf W. Larson, Director, National Council for Accreditation of Teacher Education

Edward C. Pomeroy, Executive Secretary, American Association of Colleges for Teacher Education

Robert Poppendieck, Specialist for Teacher Education, U. S. Office of Education

Staff

Don Davies, Executive Secretary

Dirck W. Brown, Associate Secretary

D. D. Darland, Associate Secretary

Roy A. Edelfelt, Associate Secretary

Edna N. Frady, Administrative Assistant

Geraldine E. Pershing, Publications Production Editor

Betty Andrews, Program Assistant

Barbara Gladysiewicz, Program Assistant

Contents

Introduction

This book is an attempt to gather together for teacher education seniors and graduates on the doorstep of the profession some of what a teacher needs to know, sense, and feel. It deals largely with Negro children (although other minority groups are both included and implied), because they are the "new problem" when school systems desegregate. They are the ones teachers are now striving to integrate.

A large percentage of the children being moved out of segregated schools are from lower-socioeconomic-class families. Their ancestors and parents have suffered from limitations imposed upon them by the institutions of discrimination in our society. The children are being described by educators as economically deprived, socially disadvantaged, and therefore unready for the middle-class public school.

Many teachers, the large majority of whom are middle class, have had no contact with lower-class Negro life or the lives of Spanish-speaking, Oriental, Indian, or Appalachian peoples. They know about the city slums, the poverty-stricken Appalachians, and the rural South, but for most of them, the only experience they have had has been to ride through those areas. Now when they face the necessity of teaching those kinds of children and of dealing with their parents, many feel more or less panic stricken. They say, "I don't know them. I don't like them. How can I teach them?"

Teachers, like all people, have prejudices. A negative prejudice is described as a complex of attitudes which predispose a person to accept a set of generalizations (or a stereotype) as characteristic of a whole group of people. For some groups, the stereotype is full of negative traits and every person in the group is prejudged accordingly. That is certainly true of the stereotype commonly applied to Negro Americans, Puerto Ricans, and Mexican-Americans. Many teachers, not having known individuals belonging to those groups, under the influence of stereotypes, imagine all kinds of difficulty in teaching their children.

ix

Segregation in every aspect of American life and the deep racist strain in our society have prevented most students, even in desegregated colleges, from coming to know Negroes of all social classes. Moreover, teacher preparation has not generally provided them with the necessary information and insight through courses in sociology, anthropology, and race or intergroup relations. Nor has the curriculum included enough actual experiences with children of different social class, racial, and ethnic groups to make the graduate feel comfortable about teaching in center-city schools.

One very serious problem for teachers is their lack of information about the complex of elements called intelligence. The Negro stereotype is based partly on the myth of racial mental inferiority. Dr. Thomas Pettigrew of Harvard has been especially helpful in refuting the charge of inferiority, in his lectures, articles, and books. A summary and quotations from his writings are included in the answer offered to the question raised by teachers, "What is the relation between race and intelligence?" The information and insight Dr. Pettigrew gives must certainly challenge teachers to do all they can to prevent and remove blocks to learning which, in their classrooms, hinder the development of nonwhite children.

Included in the answers to the question about race and intelligence are sections taken from a declaration about race and biology made by scientists from all relevant fields, in a meeting convened by UNESCO, and answers to specific questions about material which purports to prove that Negroes are innately inferior.

In answer to the question, "Isn't much talent going to waste?" we included "Our Wasted Potential," an article by Dr. Daniel Thompson, sociologist at Dillard University in New Orleans. This describes some of the social and family conditions that impinge upon lower-class Negro school children. It will help the young teacher to prepare to meet Negro parents.

Most of Dr. Robert Coles' article, "It's the Same, but It's Different," which reflects his study of Southern Negroes, has been used to answer the question, "What is the meaning of skin color to Negro children?" It provides insight into how the experiences of some Southern Negroes have affected their personalities, their philosophy of life, and their behavior patterns.

The how-to-do-it sections of this book are intended to help prospective teachers apply new information, awareness, sensitivity, and insight to specific day-by-day situations that will confront them as soon as they step into the classroom. While writing them I kept in mind the cry of many young teachers: "Why didn't someone tell me?" The stories I have used are true. Most are things I actually saw or heard in a classroom. They illustrate what not to do; what hurts Negro and other minority group children (and whites); what blocks learning by creating anxiety or fear or anger, or confirms feelings of inferiority, or supports negative prejudice and rejection on the part of white classmates. Most of the teachers in these stories were not aware of the import of their words and actions. When I have told them to teachers, they have served to create awareness and deepen sensitivity.

The objective of the entire book is to help teachers to move from desegregation (which is merely physical placement of children) to integration. Racial integration cannot be defined simply. To my mind, it is a state of being which exists when people of both (or all) races accept themselves and each other, recognize the value of their differences, and know the contributions both groups have and should be enabled to make to the common good. People can move toward integration when they realize that they have prejudices and tendencies to use stereotypes and are willing to subject those prejudgments and generalizations to reality testing. School integration exists when teachers and pupils exercise their own civil and human rights and privileges and demand that everyone else be allowed his rights and privileges. Especially in school, integration means that high value is placed on the individual and on human life and that all strive for the full development of the unknown potentialities of every child.

The book presents a specific, positive point of view with respect to race, race relations, and integration in education. It does not temporize with the moral issue, nor does it make any pretense of presenting both sides of matters that some people may regard as controversial. The writers have long been among those who have stood up to be counted in the American struggle for civil rights and equality of educational opportunity. It is their hope that the young men and women for whom the book is written and to whom it is dedicated will find in it enough information and insight to enable them, too, to make a firm commitment to democratic education for all the children of all the people.

In his address at Howard University last year, President Lyndon B. Johnson said that "the task is to give twenty million Negroes the same choice as every other American to learn and work and share in society, to develop their abilities—physical, mental, and spiritual—and to pursue their individual happiness."

Teachers have the responsibility for meeting that challenge in the beginning—childhood.

Gertrude Noar

A Child Went Forth

There was a child went forth every day,
And the first object he look'd upon, that object he became,
And that object became part of him.

. . . the school mistress that passed on her way to the school,
And the friendly boys . . . and the quarrelsome boys,
And the tidy girls and the . . . Negro boy and girl.

These became part of that child who went forth every day,
    and who now goes, and will always go forth every day.

Walt Whitman

Welcome to our classroom

The classroom was crowded and noisy, irksome with the smell of small children not too well washed. Joyce Brown, the teacher, was flushed and harried in her efforts to get things going. Suddenly the door was pulled open by Mrs. Williams, the office secretary, and a small brown boy was pushed into the room. To be heard above the noise, Mrs. Williams shrilled, "Miss J., here's a new one for you," and the door slammed shut.

Miss J. took one look and, loudly enough to be heard by all, burst out in a voice filled with frustration, "Oh, no! No! Not another!" Then catching hold of his shoulder, she pushed the child against the front chalkboard, saying, "Well, stand there till I decide where to put you." He stood there, terrified and forgotten until, when all the rest had gone out to play, Miss J. saw him again, as if for the first time.

A new building, harsh voices, impatient questioning, long waiting in the office for his turn to be registered by a white adult, a sea of children's faces—all white, it seemed—an unwelcoming teacher, a long time to stand alone, and no one to call him by name. What a way to begin life as part of the mainstream of America's school children. What feelings of guilt will nag Miss J. when, reviewing her day, she tries to get to sleep on the night of her first day in a desegregated school? What can she ever do to achieve integration in her classroom? Try not to let that happen to you, whether you are a white teacher receiving Negro children or a Negro teacher receiving white children, when you go to teach in any one of the desegregated schools which will increase in numbers in the city, suburban, and rural school districts across the nation. Be ready to receive the newcomers.

1

Perhaps the first thing to do is to understand and accept the fact that every new child must be placed in a classroom no matter how many others are already there. He has a legal and moral right to be there. He, personally, is not to blame if he wasn't there when the bell rang to begin the day. So you, the teacher, must welcome him and he must know that you do. If he is little, take his hand; if he is older, extend your hand for a warm, reassuring handshake. If the secretary failed to tell you his name, ask him and then introduce him to his classmates. Your tone of voice, inflection, the words you use, the quality of your smile, your gesture, and the warmth of your hand will tell him whether or not you accept him. The other children in the room will sense your feelings toward him and imitate you.

Even in a crowded classroom, the Negro newcomer, like any other child, must have a place to sit and to work. He should not be placed alone, up front at the table. He should not be given the last seat in the last row—a place which connotes rejection or failure in the minds of many pupils. If he comes on any other than the first day, you should already know someone in the group willing to be his pal, alongside of whom he can sit, who will show him the ropes throughout the day, take him to the bathroom and to the play area, and be with him at lunchtime.

Remember that the newcomer in a previously all Negro school may be a white child. Everything said so far applies equally to how he should be welcomed and taken care of by teacher and classmates.

Where shall I put them?

The visitor who had come to see how desegregation was working was seated at the back of the room. She had located two Negro boys in the group of twenty-five fifth-graders. Mrs. Green, the teacher, who had come back to sit beside her, was ready to answer questions, so the visitor began with, "How do you arrange the seating, Mrs. Green?"

"Oh," said the teacher, "I let them sit where they want to." Then she became aware that the last boy in the middle row, directly in front of her, was Negro. She began to tap him on the back with her pencil, saying, "Now this one just came, so I took a girl out of here, who needed help, and brought her up near my desk. That left this place for him." Then looking around her room, Mrs. Green saw that the other Negro boy was the last child in the last row. Turning to the visitor, she said, "Now that one is there because he tends to the windows." (The visitor had previously seen a white boy tending to the windows.) What was wrong here?

Mrs. Green failed to refer to Negro children by name. She said "this one" and "that one." She tapped a child on the back and talked about him as if he had no sense of touch and did not hear. The visitor had an uncomfortable feeling that to Mrs. Green these two boys were not quite human. Mrs. Green seemed not to know that a newcomer, especially a Negro child in an almost entirely white group, would need help and, above all, would be grateful for the security that comes from sitting near the teacher's desk.

Teachers use many ways of arranging children in the classroom. What you do will depend upon the kind of furniture, the procedures established in the school, and your own command of yourself and the situation. In desegregated schools, it is essential

that the method you choose should not distinguish Negro children from white ones. Perhaps the safest way for you to begin the year is to seat the pupils in alphabetical order, explaining to the children that the arrangement will help you to get to know their names. You may at once see that a small child at the back is hidden by a large one, and that his seat needs to be changed at once for that reason. Another child who tells you (or whose medical record shows) he has hearing or vision defects may need to be placed near the front of the room.

When you know the children you will want to vary the seating patterns from time to time. Sometimes you can let the pupils decide where they want to sit—up front, in the middle, at the back, near the windows, near the boards. You must make sure that this is not done in terms of whom to sit beside, lest the Negro children become isolated or segregated.

When you rearrange for small group work, be sure the Negro children are mixed in with the white ones. If chairs are arranged in circles for some activities, be sure there is room for all and that Negro children are not crowded out. If you teach little children, when they sit on the floor around you to hear a story or to sing, be sure that the Negro children are not out on the fringes. As often as possible, one, at least, should be placed close to you.

Sometimes in newly desegregated schools, a child (usually at his parents' insistence) will refuse to sit next to a Negro. If the seating is alphabetical, you can say, "That is where you belong and everyone else is where he belongs." In such cases, no changes should be attempted until the children have lost their feelings of difference. Should a single child disturb the group with continued refusal to remain in his place for this same reason, let him sit alone, apart from the group, until he is ready to return to his assigned seat. Usually children hate isolation and in order to be back in the group quickly conform to the necessary conditions.

Do not assume or accept the idea that "they (meaning Negro children) like to be with their own." It is true that any person feels more secure when he is near his friends. However, there is no reason to suppose that similarity in skin color means that children know or like each other. Moreover, integration requires you to use every means at your disposal to give your pupils experience across race lines so that racial difference ceases to be a valid reason for rejection. Seating helps. Among the arrangements to be avoided are one row white, the next Negro; Negroes on one side of the room, whites on the other (with or without a vacant row between); whites at the front of the room, Negroes at the back (or vice versa); girls up front, boys at the rear; a Negro child seated alone with empty chairs on either side of him.

If white children are in the minority in a classroom, they are likely to play minority group roles. You, then, will need to pay attention to where they sit, to keep them in the group, to make sure they are not on the fringes.

Oriental children now suffer less from rejection than they used to. Moreover, the common stereotype of them contains few negative elements. One of the greatest hazards for them, especially when very few are enrolled, because they are often attractive, clean, quiet, and studious, is the mascot role. If teachers or pupils are prejudiced against them, everything in this section and all that follows will apply in equal measure.

Of course I like them

Do you? Then be sure your Negro, Oriental, Mexican-American, Indian, and Puerto Rican as well as your white children know it. If you are nonwhite, be sure you communicate acceptance to your white pupils. The most basic need which every human being has throughout life is to be accepted for himself alone, regardless of what makes him different from others. Desegregation poses a special challenge to teachers who must assure Negro children that they are wanted and needed, that they are liked and respected, that they belong.

In spite of the 1964 Civil Rights Act, in many school systems Negroes are still excluded from rooms in which there are white children and teachers. In other places they come into their new schools fully aware that teachers joined with the parents of their new classmates in unseemly demonstrations against desegregation. In some communities they still have to walk through lines of jeering adults and children who call them names, spit upon them, and threaten bodily harm. And even if none of this may have occurred in the school district to which you are assigned, your Negro pupils are upset by the fact that it is happening elsewhere to children like themselves and for no reason other than skin color.

In order to achieve integration you must understand the racial experience of rejection—what it does to the Negro's self-image, how it may prevent him from achieving a warm relationship with you (if you are white) and block his efforts to establish his place in the peer group. You also have to root out from the depths of your own mind and heart all vestiges of racism and replace the myth of racial superiority with the fact that, as far as potentiality is concerned, all races are equal. Only then will you be able to communicate to the Negro child that you, his teacher, do sincerely accept him and intend that in your classroom he shall have equal opportunity to be and to become. The pupils in your room will watch your behavior closely to see whether your deeds match your words. Most of them will follow your lead, especially if they like you and accept you as a role model.

You will communicate acceptance to pupils different from yourself by what you say and how you say it, by your tone of voice and inflection, by the expression on your face, by your gestures and the quality of your contact when you touch them. A classroom incident showed one teacher how especially sensitive her children were to the nonverbal means of communication she unconsciously used. Several Negro children lingered by Mrs. Carpenter's desk at the close of the afternoon session. After chatting with them about the project under way, she said, "You children think I don't like you, don't you?"

She had hoped they would say no, but one slowly and sadly answered, "Yes, we do."

"What makes you think so?" the teacher asked.

A second child said, "Because when you touch us you shiver!"

Look how nonverbal communication figures in the following story. A group of Negro teen-agers were talking to the social worker assigned to visit their homes. "We aren't doing too well," said Sandra.

"Why not?" the visitor asked.

"You see," said Jean, "the teachers pass us by too quickly. They ask a question, then shrug their shoulders or raise their eyebrows, and we know they think we are stupid, so we just sit down."

Then Mike spoke up. "I was absent for a week. When I got back I stopped at Mr. Roberts' desk to ask where I should sit and what I was to do. His face got red, he banged on the desk, shook his finger at me and yelled, 'Don't bother me now. I have more important things to do then tend to you.' I just turned on my heel and walked out again."

Every teacher must have a way of taking care of returning absentees regardless of the cause of absence. A good plan will also help to create integration. For example, have able children, both Negro and white, take turns being class secretary for the week. Then after saying, "I'm glad you are back, we missed you," you can say to a returning pupil, "Go sit with Marie (regardless of color). She has the class log (or diary) and will tell you what we did while you were gone." Perhaps, if you keep the absentee in mind, you can add, "We formed committees last week and saved a place for you in Edward's group (again regardless of color), so go to him to find out what his group is planning to do. Then, if you think that isn't what you want to do, you can come talk it over with me."

In that way you not only tell the child that he was worth remembering, but you also give him the same opportunity to participate in decision making that all the rest of the pupils had. A child who knows he is accepted and has equality of status in the classroom usually does not want to stay away from school.

When speaking of their Negro children, teachers in newly desegregated schools sometimes say, "They would be happier in their own school. They aren't happy here." An unhappy child, whether he is anxious or lonely, will have learning difficulty. The teacher, being responsible for removing whatever blocks learning, is obligated to discover the causes of unhappiness in any child, regardless of his skin color. Children of all groups are happy in school when they know they belong and are accepted and wanted in the room, when they are successful and receive rewards for work well done.

What did I say?

Many color words in the English language arouse emotions because they have value undertones which are internalized by non-white children. Teachers often are not aware of this. In desegregated schools, therefore, they must learn about those words and help the children to know that they do not necessarily refer to themselves. *Black, brown* and *colored* are among the words to watch, as the following incidents show.

• The third-grade class was busy with brushes and paints. Miss Jones was moving around the room giving suggestions and helping children learn how to mix colors. She came to Johnny and in passing said, "Don't use black, John. It's so ugly." Johnny was a very dark-skinned child.

• Christmas was only a week away and the children were busy making decorations. Some had cut out stenciled angels and were coloring them. Brown-skinned Billy finished his first and proudly took it to the teacher to hang on the tree. "Oh, no!" said Miss White. "I can't use that one, Billy. Angels are white. Do another."

• Mrs. Martin, with sudden insight and some horror at her own lack of awareness, said, "My goodness, I've been using colors to grade my children's papers. I used a black crayon for the lowest mark a youngster could get."

• Susie was confused. She didn't understand what to do next, so she went up to the teacher, who said, "Go get some paper."

"What paper, where?" asked the child.

"Over there are the colored papers."

"No, no," wailed Susie. "I want to use the same paper the white kids use."

• "Jack, if you don't stop that now," said Miss McKay, "I'll put you on my blacklist."

"Hey, Miss McKay," called honey-colored Tim, "what can I do to get on your white list?"

Some of the above stories tell how easy it is to violate the Negro child's sense of self-worth. In each case the teacher's use of the word *black* also served to support whatever prejudices and negative stereotypes of Negroes the white children may have had.

From earliest childhood both brown and white children associate black and brown with ink and soil. If one gets inky or dirty he is called naughty. Black is associated with fear and even with the devil. By association and because of attitudes often unconsciously communicated to them by significant adults, white children may come to see dark-skinned people as fearsome and even bad. Teachers must help them to know that brown and black things and people as well as light-colored things and people can be, and often are, pleasant, good, lovely, and friendly. For example, though the darkness of night can be sinister, it also brings the beauty of moonlight and stars.

Negro children are likely to internalize the negative values when *black* is used to mean evil and fear and when *brown* only means the soil or dirt. They have to learn that they are not the targets of abuse every time color words are used. Teachers aware of the dangers make special efforts to prevent them from developing feelings of self-hate and inferiority.[1]

Many white children and adults are addicted to stereotypic thinking. In every stereotype there is an insulting name, the use of which causes anger and anguish. In your desegregated school you will undoubtedly hear teachers and children use the name "nigger," or in the South, "nigra." Negroes also use derogatory names for white people, like "soda cracker," or "Mr. Charlie," or "the man," or "ofay." You cannot regard name-calling as trivial. If your children are little, you must talk with them about it. If you have an older group, you should have a unit on stereotypes. A most fruitful experience in such a study will be testing common racial, religious, and ethnic group characterizations, both negative and positive, against the reality of people the pupils know.

In secondary schools, a unit on prejudice can be introduced in language arts or social studies. It involves elements of mental health: the effect of hatred on the self and a chance to talk about how it hurts to be left out or rejected. Name-calling, scapegoating,

---

[1]Goodman, Mary Ellen. *Race Awareness in Young Children.* Revised edition. New York: Collier Books, 1964.

rejection, exclusion, and violence are the ways people act out various degrees of prejudice common in both child and adult society.

Units on values, race relations, or intergroup relations give teen-agers a chance to identify their own value patterns and correct misconceptions about the values of people different from themselves. They learn how values are transmitted to children and come to understand the role that values play in making decisions about how to act and how to treat other people.

I can't communicate with these children

It was faculty meeting time in a newly desegregated school. A consultant had come from the university to help the teachers identify and solve their problems. Mrs. Sullivan spoke up first, saying, "I just can't communicate with these children."

"Yes, that's right," another added. "It's a matter of communication. We don't understand them."

For awhile it seemed that the trouble was the Negro children's use of idioms and colloquialisms. For example, the teachers did not understand why fights began when one child accused another, saying, "He called me out of my name," or because someone said, "Your mother" (which implied sex behavior on her part).

Then Mr. Miller said, "But it's not that so much as that the children don't seem to know what I say. Yesterday I was talking about foods and I mentioned the avocado. They never heard of it, so I tried alligator pear. That didn't work either, so today I brought one in, cut it open, and let them taste it. They didn't like it."

"I had an experience too," said Mrs. Johnson. "Several times, as they were going out I said, 'Single file.' They smiled at me and went on out in twos and threes. Then I said, 'Now get one behind the other and make one line.' They obeyed me without any trouble at all."

A teacher in an Eastern city junior high school was discussing problems of living together in her room. She invited the pupils to tell what they would like each other and her to do differently in order to be happier together. One child said, "Sometimes you say, 'Oh, fiddlesticks.' We don't know what that means."

Another agreed and added, "Then you say just 'Oh.'"

A third spoke up, "And sometimes you just look and don't say anything!"

In a Midwestern city, small pupils were asked what a teacher could do to make them feel that she liked and respected them. Among their most frequent answers were, "Smile at us," "Let us go to the bathroom," and "Please tell her not to holler at us!"

Communication is a two-way problem. It is evident that some of the trouble may lie with the teacher. If he forgets that lower-socioeconomic-class children, both Negro and white, have vocabulary limitations, he is likely to use words, phrases, and expressions with which they have had no experience. Also, their parents do not engage them in the kind of language feedback, correction, and vocabulary enlargement that occurs in middle-class families. Nothing about this is purely racial. However, because more Negroes than whites have suffered from the limitations of poverty, in center-city classrooms and in Southern rural areas they are more likely to have language disadvantages. If you want to give Negro pupils in your room equal opportunity to learn (which integration demands), you must simplify your language, strive to express ideas in several different ways, and provide experiences when it is obvious that concepts behind word symbols are missing.

Some idioms and colloquialisms are racial, in which case the white children as well as you, yourself, may not know their meaning. In like manner you may have difficulty understanding teen-age slang, jive, hep-talk, and other jargons that change so rapidly it is hard for adults to keep up with them. You can treat the problem quite cavalierly and have fun with it. The Negro and white children can exchange idiomatic expressions with you and each other, learning each other's language, so to speak. You, however, have responsibility for teaching suitability and good taste. You teach all the children that some kinds of language patterns may be OK for them to use in the neighborhood but not in school if they want to be accepted by classmates. Assimilation into middle-class life may depend upon using correct grammar, which is also needed when applying for, holding, and advancing in various kinds of occupations.

When some teachers anticipate classroom desegregation, they worry about the use of obscenity and profanity. You may be one who believes that Negro children use four-letter words and swear more than white children do. Unseemly language is not connected with race but rather with social class. A pupil who uses bad language in the classroom needs to learn that it offends and will cause him to be rejected by some of his classmates. However, you, the teacher, must control your own tendency to feel insulted by bad language. No teacher ever needs to think less well of himself because a child swears at him or calls him names. This is not to imply that you should ignore such impulsive or deliberate attempts to dominate you. Before dealing with the offense, however, you must find out whether or not the child knows the meaning of the words he used.

Teachers handle the use of bad language in various ways. Jimmy, in the kindergarten, was playing with a toy. Suddenly he ripped out an oath, "You blank . . . ."

The teacher, hearing it, said, "Jimmy, what does that mean?"

The child looked up and, smiling sweetly, said, "It means the car won't start." Obviously no action was required on the teacher's part.

Miss White was attempting to correct one of her more difficult adolescents. He called her a liar. She replied, quite calmly, "No, I'm not."

Mr. Smith threatened Sam with dire punishment if he continued to disturb the class. Exasperated, Sam muttered, "Aw, go to hell."

Unperturbed, Mr. Smith replied, "I don't have to."

By maintaining a calm manner and a quiet voice, and by clearly indicating to a pupil that he cannot bully or insult you or dominate the classroom, you will retain control of the situation and thus defeat the child who wants to get control over you, make you blow up, and thus entertain the class. The pupils eagerly listen in to such exchanges to see who wins. If the perpetrator is defeated, he loses face, often breaks down, and thus at a later time, when you get him by himself, he is open to correction of his behavior.

Teachers have language patterns which children may have some trouble getting used to. One of these is the distortion of questions. For example, a teacher working with a class on arithmetic said, "We must watch our what?" Another one, in a junior high school, dictating test questions which required pupils to fill in blank spaces, said, "The what stands for the what which means what when it is combined with what to form what?" Such questions are bad English. Moreover, they call for one-word answers which may or may not be in every child's vocabulary.

A very great hazard for the lower-socioeconomic-class children is the direction to perform in relation to something quite outside their experience. For example, a child was unable to put anything on his paper when told to paint a Maypole. He wasn't even able to remember the word itself, let alone draw what he had never seen.

14

Who is he? Why is he here? Where is he going?

Everyone, at some time, asks such questions about the identity of another person, and more important for teachers, every teen-ager seeks answers to the same questions about himself. His search for his own identity is made more difficult if the kinds of experiences which help him to know himself have been missing in his early childhood. For example, many children live in poverty-stricken homes in which parents, preoccupied with their own work and anxieties, pay little attention to building up a child's personality. Consequently some children, at four or five, do not know their own names and have never seen their own faces in mirrors which do not distort their features. It helps them to know and like their own faces when classrooms are equipped with good mirrors.

Preschool, kindergarten, and first-grade teachers usually print the children's names on large pieces of paper which can then be tied on as hats or pinned on as belts or used as name tags. All teachers should avoid calling Negro children "boy" or "girl." One teacher was quite upset when, not intending harm, she called to a child, "Boy, you boy, come here."

The child turned on her with anger, and said, "My name is Raymond; you use it!"

In slavery and thereafter in the South, depriving Negroes of names was a device used to deny them the right to personal worth and identity. Even today it is not unusual to hear a white Southerner call to a Negro man, "Come here, boy," which he rightfully regards as an insult. The use of courtesy titles—Mrs., Mr., and Miss —and of last names is essential to establish good interpersonal, interracial relations. Negro women teachers often call each other by their last names. Both Negro men and women teachers tend to use the courtesy titles and last names for secondary school students.

Negroes are sometimes unduly sensitive and may see insult when none is intended. In discussing how teachers might be chosen to pioneer in faculty desegregation, a speaker said, "The superintendent might say to you 'You're just the right gal for that school.'" A member of the audience was upset about the use of the familiar term "gal," yet in the particular situation it meant only full recognition of the teacher's appropriate personality and qualifications.

15

The camera is another device you can use to help children get used to seeing and taking pride in themselves and their appearance. Many children never have had their pictures taken. The snapshots you take will please them, especially if they are enlarged and mounted in simulated frames. After being displayed, each photo should be given to the pictured child. It is especially important to take pictures of children at work, for example, reading, painting, or play-acting. Children take great pride in the identification of self with school tasks and love to point to those pictures on PTA nights and visiting days, saying, for example, "Look, Mom, that's me painting."

The face most assuredly pictures the self and therefore teachers must be very careful not to disparage it. This writer heard one angry teacher scream at a misbehaving pupil, "Get out of here! I can't stand looking at your face any longer!" That teacher struck at the roots of that child's self. She should not have been surprised when he refused to return to her classroom. The insult was doubly compounded by the fact that the child had brown skin.

When you do not like a child's behavior, it is essential for you to tell him so. You may even try to make him ashamed of his actions. But behavior is not the self. It is better to say, "You I like. But I do not like what you *do,* and you must change your way of acting (or speaking)."

It is also very important for you to avoid saddling a Negro child, or one from any other minority group, with guilt for shaming his race or his religious (or nationality) group, or even his family. For example, do not say, "Your family will suffer from what you have done," or "You are dragging down your whole race," or "The Irish will be ashamed of you." This is entirely too heavy a load for any child to bear. Moreover, a pupil's in-school behavior rarely brings such dire consequences.

In our society a person's work often seems to symbolize himself. We ask, "What *is* he?" when we mean, "What does he *do?*" The answer, "He is a doctor," for example, establishes the person's high professional status. We also may answer the question, "Who is he?" by indicating his material possessions—"He is a millionaire." That establishes his high socioeconomic status. The answer, "He is a Negro," may indicate that the person is more or less preoccupied with race alone.

Many lower-socioeconomic-class Negro children have neither material possessions nor aspirations for future status positions. You may be able to provide some books and tools for them to own, at least for the duration of the school year. You can find many opportunities to inform them about the kinds of jobs now open to all who qualify. Take every chance you can to test and evaluate and help each one to recognize his strengths and weaknesses in terms of what various kinds of work and professions require. Help each one to eliminate his weaknesses and capitalize on his strengths.

Realistic self-appraisal is essential. But remember that you do not know what the potentialities for development are. Some children are slow-growers or late-bloomers. Negro children, benefiting from new hope and the new environment, are likely to show abilities neither you nor they suspected they had. Poverty-stricken Negro parents who are hopeless because of discriminatory unemployment rarely ask their young ones, "What are you going to be when you grow up?" They and their children have little reason to believe that in a democracy a person has the right to become something of his own choosing.

Because the struggle to find the wherewithal needed to survive from day to day is so intense, many lower-class parents and children do not learn to withhold gratification of present desires in terms of future goals. Little children who have not been so trained will, for example, want to eat as soon as they are hungry. You may have to find someplace where all lunch bags can be stored so the food can be saved for lunchtime.

Do not be misled by the quality of the clothing a child wears to school into believing that the family's income is adequate. In some communities, organizations that are anxious to make children who pioneer as comfortable as possible provide clothing for them. The dresses and suits the pupils wear to school are often taken off as soon as school is over, washed and pressed so as to be spotless for the next day. Investigation of home conditions and of the parents' employment and income levels may reveal that some well-dressed children live in poverty-stricken homes.

Lawrence K. Frank said that "the child . . . must create for himself, out of his experiences and the teaching he receives, an image of himself and of the kind of person he would like to be. This ideal of self will embody all the feelings of inadequacy and guilt that the child has experienced and must somehow express. . . . Undoubtedly the largest single element . . . is the kind and extent of affectionate personal interest shown by an adult toward the child, who thereby may find much needed help toward a constructive, not a self-defeating, ideal of self."[1]

---

[1]*The Fundamental Needs of the Child.* Columbus, Ohio: Charles E. Merrill. New edition projected for 1966.

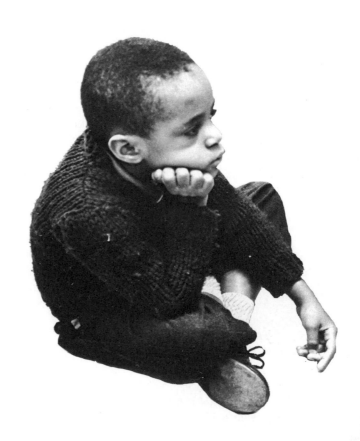

Who Am I?[1]

by Theron Jacobson, Primary Teacher
Washington School
Decatur, Illinois

I am Negro—
    I am bad.
I am poor white trash—
    I am bad.
My mother whips me to make me good—
    I am bad.
My preacher says the devil will get me—
    I am bad.
Jesus don't love me—
    I am bad.
I don't know what that teacher says—
    I am bad.
I don't understand her so I don't listen—
    I am bad.
I don't know them funny black marks in my book—
    I am bad.
I can't make them marks stay on the lines—
    I am bad.
My teacher puts a paper on my desk—
    I don't know what to do—
    I do nothin'—
        I am bad.
I make pretty colored marks on the paper (I like my crayons)—
    It makes me feel good—
    I want to show it to the kid next to me and tell him about it—
    I talked—
    I marked up my paper—
        I am very, very bad.
That kid next to me—he is good—
    The teacher likes his paper—
    He went to play with some trucks and blocks—
    I want to play with blocks and trucks—
        No! I am bad.

---

[1]From *Educational Leadership* 23: 121-23; November 1965. Reproduced by permission of the author and the publisher, the Association for Supervision and Curriculum Development, Washington, D. C.

I marked up my paper—
> *Blocks and trucks are for good kids—*
> *Bad boys put their heads on their desks—*
>> *I am very bad.*

I don't feel good—
> *I made marks on that kid's paper and threw it on the floor—*
> *It made me feel good—*
>> *Now I am very, very bad.*

The bell rings—
> *I can go!*

Who am I?
I run—
I shout—
I hit that kid next to me—
I am Negro—
I am poor white trash—
I don't know nothin'—
I don't listen—
I am lazy—
I don't sit still—
I mark on my papers—
I mark on other kids' papers—
I hit kids—
I know who I am—
I am the bad-dest kid in the room—
Everybody knows it—
> *I am so bad.*

Today the teacher smiled at me!
> *"Hello—I like that red shirt!"*
> *I don't say nothin'!—*
> *I see some trucks—*
> *I'd like to roll them on the rug—*
> *She don't care—*
> *I roll them and roll them—*
>> *That makes me feel real good.*

I'll take them blocks and make me a garage for my trucks—
> *I make me a good garage and put my trucks in it—*
> *I lie on the rug and look at it—*
>> *I feel good.*

My teacher says, "Tony, you made a good garage.
   You used some red blocks.
   Let's count together and see how many red blocks you used.
   1—2—3—4.
   Let's see how many wheels are on that truck.
   1—2—3—4.
   Tony, you are a smart boy!
   You can count!"
      I feel very, very good!

That kid next to me—
   He wanted to make a garage too—
   I helped him—
   We made a garage—
   It was a big garage—
   We put a big truck in it—
   That boy said we had 2 garages and 2 trucks—
   We used some green blocks—
   That boy and me counted—
   He helped me count 8 green blocks—
      I feel good!

We got some paper—
   A big stack is over there where we can get it anytime we
         want it—
   We made big colored marks all over our papers—
      It looked pretty!
   My teacher said, "Tony and Jeff, you made some
         pretty pictures!
   Get that roll of tape and we'll put them up.
   I'll write your names with my big black pencil so everyone
         can see!
   We have 2 pretty pictures!"
      I feel good.
   Them funny marks says my name—
      I believe I can make one of them funny marks—
   I made one on the board—
      I feel good.

My teacher said, "My, that is good!
   Some of these days you can write all your name.
   You are a smart boy.
   I'm glad you are in my room!"
      She likes me!

21

I say, "I'll make you 'nuther good picture, better 'n that!"
Me and that kid next to me went out to play.
   He likes me!

Who am I?

I am a boy—
   I am good!
I am Tony—
   I am good!
I made a good garage—
   I am good!
I counted—
   I am good!
I know this is a red shirt—
   I am good!
That kid likes me—
   I am good!
The teacher likes me—
   I am good!
I made a pretty picture—
   I am good!
I know them funny marks says my name—
   I am good!
I made one of them marks—
   I am very, very good!
That kid next to me is good, too—
We're 2 good boys—
   I'm glad I'm me!

Are "they" really what "they" seem to be?

Teachers who are unfamiliar with lower-socioeconomic living conditions often misjudge the children of poverty and tend to blame the parents for what they do not like in their pupils. Three hundred years of limitation, restriction, discrimination, and segregation have kept a disproportionately large number of Negro families in the slums. Their children have suffered not only from lack of money, food, and clothing, but also from denial of access to the resources, facilities, and opportunities for learning experiences that exist in most communities. Although outlawed by the Civil Rights Act of 1964, denials persist in many Northern and Southern communities. Moreover, many Negroes cannot avail themselves of cultural opportunities that are open to them, because they lack the price of admission or transportation.

The early years of poverty-stricken children are often barren of what we call "culture"—stories, poems, books, pictures, and everything out-of-doors except the streets on which they live. They also have had little help from adults in learning words and concepts, in classifying and generalizing. Their audio and visual perceptions are likely to be underdeveloped, but they have learned to screen out voices from the mixture of sounds around them. The behavior patterns they had to learn in order to survive often give teachers concern and are often mislabeled by them.

Keep in mind that the following descriptions of what the so-called slum children are like in school are not related to race as such but rather are ways in which many *lower-social-class* white and Negro children act. In America we have both middle- and upper-class Negro families whose value and behavior patterns do not differ from middle- and upper-class white patterns. Unless you have deep racial prejudices, you will find their children as easy to

23

like, respect, and teach as white middle-class children. Remember also that the descriptions which follow do not apply to *every poor child.* You will need to guard against using them as a stereotype.

Children are individuals, no matter where they come from or what their race or social class may be. You must study each child and learn to judge each one on the basis of his worth as a human being. You must regard each one as the possessor of unknown potential, the development of which is your responsibility and your challenge.

One behavior pattern which is often called *babyish* includes uncontrolled talking, playing, tapping of pencils and feet, eating and crying. The cause may be the child's need to move around. He may be unaccustomed to sitting still for any length of time; he may be irked by the closeness of desk to chair, of child to child. He usually is *frustrated* rather than immature.

Some of the children we are talking about get *angry* over what they are expected to endure or at the brusk, loud tones teachers

sometimes use to give orders. Anger is also directed at self when efforts to do a difficult task or to keep up with classmates are futile. Do not err by calling such children *uncontrollable*.

Little Negro children, especially, may be afraid. From early childhood on, *fear* of white people is often an intimate part of their lives. In the mixed classroom they are also afraid of ridicule and reprisal if what they say is wrong or displeases the teacher or peers. Fear may cause a child to answer sharply or use a querulous tone of voice. Do not hastily accuse such a child of *impudence*.

Negro children who have not previously been in mixed classes are likely to *underachieve* partly because of their lack of experience with competition as a way of life, partly because they are unaccustomed to speed exercises and time requirements. Do not prejudge those children to be *uncooperative* or *lacking in ambition*.

Poor children in large families very often have nothing to call their very own. They may not understand the *concept of private property*. Whatever the family affords, whether it be food, clothing, or school supplies, belongs to all and each takes what he needs from the common supply. These children may take pencils, paper, or even books from the boxes or closets in which they are stored. Be not quick to accuse them of *stealing*. Withhold the label, too, when a child eats a classmate's lunch; he may be very hungry. If a rejected child takes another's belongings, it may be a signal that he is lonely and needs relationship.

Negro children in desegregated classrooms sometimes are suspicious, especially of children who offer friendship and of teachers who do not convey sincerity. In teachers' words, they "carry a chip on their shoulders," or "constantly complain of being picked on," or "are hostile," or "pull away when I touch them." Do not be in a hurry to consider them *neurotic* as some teachers claim. In all probability they have not yet had enough experience with white people to be *comfortable*.

Teachers worry a great deal over *fighting*. They see Negro children fight with each other even more than with whites. Sometimes in their anxiety they even encourage children to tell on each other about fighting in the neighborhood on the way to and from school. Do not make the mistake of thinking this means that Negroes are *hostile* or *brutal* or *ugly* and to be feared. Remember that middle- as well as lower-class white parents are proud when their boys come home with black eyes as long as they beat up the other kid. In lower-class life, children are necessarily taught that they must *stand up for themselves and protect themselves as well as their brothers and sisters.*

25

Negro children seem to teachers to be *slow*. They "take their time." What is there to hurry for in their lives, in their families? They are often tardy because there is no alarm clock and no adult has to get up to go to work—they are all unemployed. Efforts to correct lateness to school by detentions or whippings fail because the children themselves are not to blame. Such a child cannot rightly be called *defiant*. He and his family simply may not be time-oriented. Be sure, too, not to call slowness *laziness* and regard it as a *racial* trait.

Disorderly desks, disorganized notebooks, pockets full of scraps of paper and bits of pencils or food do not mean that a child is disorganized or *psychotic* or personally *dirty*. If the home is crowded, lacks furniture with drawers, has few if any closets, and the single, poorly equipped bathroom has to be shared with other tenants, parents cannot teach children to be clean, orderly, and organized. Instead of blaming them and the children, put your energy into devising learning experiences which will develop the values and characteristics you want the children to have.

Poor families do not spend money for games which teach children to follow directions. Moreover, they have little need to give more than simple directions. The child is expected to do whatever he is told to do, and he is rarely praised and rewarded when he does it well. Be careful not to regard *failure to follow directions* as disobedience. Begin to teach how to do so with simple directions. As you increase their complexity, put on the board some reminders of each step so that slower children, whose anxiety to keep up may frustrate them, can follow along. Learning will be facilitated by encouragement and help and praise.

Inability to *compete* should not be dubbed *lack of interest in success* or *no ambition for the future*. Economically deprived parents do not usually buy children the kinds of games and toys which two or more people play with together to see which one wins or which one finishes first. Moreover, in life itself these children have seen that Negroes cannot win in competition with whites. One thing the integrated experience is for is to help them to have confidence in their ability to compete effectively in the mainstream of American life.

Aren't we making them unhappy?

Does everybody have to be middle class? Aren't we taking away their culture? Shouldn't we respect lower-class values? Aren't we causing conflict between parents and children when we try to change children's values? Wouldn't it be better to put good schools into the slums rather than to take the children out for a few hours and then send them back? What about culture shock? Shouldn't "they" (Negroes) pull themselves up by their bootstraps like other people did? Questions like these reveal lack of information and insight into the nature of American life.

America is called an open society. That means people are able to move up the socioeconomic-class ladder. Education has been the means of achieving social mobility, and historically the public school has been charged with responsibility for helping people to be successful in making that climb. Negro Americans who in the beginning did not choose to come but were captured and forced into slavery were at once placed on the other side of a caste wall. Schooling was denied them in slavery, and since emancipation, their schooling for the most part has remained separate and inferior. Even in the North, where housing discrimination created slum ghettos, de facto segregation kept many children in admittedly poorer schools. The facts are well documented in current writings and research reports.

Contrast what happened to Negroes with what was done for other people. America received immigrants from all over the world. Large numbers, probably most of them, came with neither money nor education, but they came of their own accord, seeking a better way of life. Community organizations and the school systems mobilized their resources to help them become "Americans." Americanization programs blossomed all over the land, but Negroes were excluded from them. Every effort was made to acculturate the newcomers, to help them assimilate (look and act like "Americans"), to give them a start up the ladder of success.

In contrast, Negroes, beginning on the slave ships, were treated with utmost brutality, were deprived of their own traditional culture patterns, and thereafter, by limitation, segregation, exclusion, and discrimination, were prevented from learning American middle-class values and behavior patterns.

Now the Negroes are demanding their human and civil rights, their civil liberties, and the first-class citizenship guaranteed to all American citizens in our basic national documents. They regard placement of their children in middle-class schools serving middle-class neighborhoods as symbolic of their final, full admission into the mainstream of American life. All public schools must now receive those children and give them what every child has the right to receive—full and equal preparation for effective living in our society. This includes teaching them the values and helping them to develop the personality characteristics and to learn whatever else is needed for success in American life.

Study of our society leads to the conclusion that middle-class ways of talking and acting and a strong drive for upward mobility are characteristic of people who do achieve the "good life," which to most people includes a high standard of living. Lower-class Negroes see this as the goal for which heretofore they were not allowed to aspire. They are determined to get full equality of opportunity for their children now.

Culture shock is a term used to describe what happens to primitive people when they are abruptly introduced to the machines and devices of modern civilization. Negro Americans are not primitives. Their families have been living here for fourteen generations. No matter how economically deprived large numbers of them may be, they still are in vicarious, if not direct, contact through films, radio, TV, and magazines with every modern device and every way of living and behaving. They have been pupils in the public schools, however inferior those schools may have been. Moreover, ever increasing numbers have been in, if not part of, the most sophisticated urban life. The ideas and concepts of modern civilization are not new to them, and their right to achieve the best that living in the United States offers can no longer be withheld. Equality of educational opportunity must be provided in every classroom.

It seems spurious indeed for teachers suddenly to argue that lower-class people like to live in depressed conditions and enjoy talking and acting only as their ancestors did in the days of a "cabin culture." The argument that middle-class schooling with middle-class white peers will produce culture shock seems to be an attempt to rationalize reluctance to integrate the schools and unwillingness to give Negro children full and equal opportunity to become socially mobile. This is not to imply that people who do not possess a strong drive for personal advancement are "bad" people.

Secondary school students, white and Negro together, need to learn about the nature of our society. Perhaps you, the teacher, may need to see (and take your social studies class to see) the wide variety of living conditions that exist in cities, suburbs, and countryside. When slums and depressed areas are visited, students should learn why people who want to have been unable to escape from the ghetto. Middle-class white pupils should know the full extent of poverty and limitation visited upon the Negro lower classes. Unless they know and understand the implications that the War on Poverty has for national survival, they will not be any better equipped to solve the nation's problems than their parents are.

The emergence of a considerable number of both middle- and upper-class Negro families testifies to the fact that the racial group itself is not lacking ability. The race is not to blame for the disproportionate number of Negroes who are both grindingly poor and culturally disadvantaged. The high academic and creative abilities of the many Negroes who have contributed to science, invention, medicine, literature, art, and music testify to the fact that intelligence and intellectual abilities are not limited to the white race. If some Negroes have not only survived the so-called culture shock but have become great people, there is no reason to suppose that exposure to middle-class value patterns in school and community will harm others.

When lower-class Negro adults, unable to get employment, have been dependent for as many as three generations, their children are not likely to place high value on time, promptness, and work. You may have to struggle to teach them, but they can and will

29

learn. When poverty and discrimination have kept families living in crowded, rat-infested cabins or tenements, often without hot water and adequate plumbing, children may not have learned to value orderliness and cleanliness and may not know how to organize the things and ideas they possess, but that does not mean they like to be dirty and disorganized. It may be hard for you to teach them, but you must find the way. Patience, encouragement, help, praise, and rewards when they succeed will bring positive results; punishment will not.

Before you prejudge them and their parents to be immoral, destructive, and violent, remember that in slavery their forebears were denied legal marriage and the sanctity of the family was violated by the white slave-owner to satisfy his own lust and greed. For generations, unions by consent were all that was expected of Negroes. This led to the matriarchal family which persists largely because the men cannot get employment and so leave the children to be supported and reared by the women. The conditions of life have led to debasement of the lower-class Negro male.

Remember, also, that these children live in the presence of violence and all their lives have come to expect violence at the hands of white people. The process of integration entrusted to you should produce for these children confidence and faith in the good will of white Americans and belief that our society will provide them with opportunities to get work and earn money commensurate with their abilities and training.

Will what you teach children to want and to do create dissatisfaction with their homes and conflict with their parents? That depends upon how you handle it. You want the children to aspire to better lives, so you must make them unhappy with their present surroundings. You teach them, of course, to dislike things and conditions, not their parents. You help them to know why their parents have been unable to get jobs and to move out of the ghettos. If conflict is the result, remember that conflict is the cutting edge of change. Without it there is no progress.

Trouble may develop if you try to teach absolute values. For example, a senior high school girl suffered emotional trauma when a teacher she admired and liked taught that people who use or sell alcoholic beverages are evil and doomed to hell-fire. Her father, whom she also admired and loved, owned and operated a tavern. Be sure you understand what the term *value* means and know how values are transmitted. Children will learn and accept for their own values held by people *they like,* people they *want to be like,* and people they want *to like them.*

30

How can I control them?

Discipline, control, giving orders, correcting, and punishing occupy much time in many classrooms regardless of the kinds of children, until the twenty-five or thirty individuals have become a group. Children must learn to respond with obedience and enough conformity to get classroom work done. The most important thing for you to do is to establish the fact that you are the teacher and that you intend to do your job.

Your first task, therefore, is to set up *the limits of behavior* in your room. If your pupils are sufficiently mature, they can and should participate in deciding what kinds of behavior are essential for good teaching and learning in their classroom. They may also help you to decide what should be the consequences of unsuitable and disrupting conduct, but they should never be involved in administering punishments. When children know the limits of behavior that adults will tolerate, they feel secure and can conform. When they do not know, they become anxious and are likely to act impulsively. Some of them may seem to go berserk!

Even when the limits are well understood, individual pupils will test them out. In one classroom, for example, a child who was at his desk doing busy work while the teacher was with a reading group made a noise by moving his chair. He looked to see if the teacher heard. She paid no attention, so he did it again. (A disapproving shake of her head would have stopped him.) Again he looked at the teacher. Still she seemed not to care, so he continued with his noise-making until the bell rang for recess.

In another class a teacher was working with a small reading group at the front of the room. She asked one child a question. While she waited for the answer, another said softly, "I know." The teacher paid no attention to this. The next question was greeted by two children, saying less softly, "I know, I know." Still the teacher did not object. With the third question came wildly waving hands and all the children shouting, "I know! I know! I know!"

31

If you have had no previous experience and hear other teachers talking about discipline, and if you tend to think about Negroes, Mexican-Americans, and Puerto Ricans in terms of the common negative stereotypes, you may be worried about how you will control them. First of all, then, you must rid yourself of the *expectation* that the Negro (or other minority group) children are going to be naughty, defiant, disobedient, and impudent. Usually, in the first months in mixed classrooms, they are quiet, try hard to follow directions, and are as polite and courteous as the best children in the room. Of course, they watch their white classmates, and in rooms where white children run around, talk back, drop books, and do other disturbing things without being corrected by the teacher, they are likely to follow suit. Then, presently, the teacher may say that she has a "Negro discipline problem," or that "the new element is troublesome." Some teachers who seem not to hear noise created by white children quickly blame the Negroes or other minority group pupils for all that goes wrong in the classroom.

Teachers report that sometimes, when they reprove or punish a Negro child, he says, "You wouldn't do that to me if I wasn't colored." This usually hurts the teacher and makes him angry. If that should happen to you, one way to deal with such a child is to remain calm while you quietly say, "I *know* how you feel. I understand *why* you feel that way, but let us look at the facts. Yesterday Andy, who is white, did the same thing you did today. How did I treat him? The same as I am treating you now." This kind of calm attempt to help a child face reality and stop being overly conscious of his race may have to be repeated until he has enough experience with you to know that you are fair and are not motivated by race prejudice.

Where physical punishment is permitted, teachers may tend to use it freely, especially on Negro or other minority group children. Some believe that lower-class children are punished only that way at home and therefore will not respond to anything else in school. It is true that in lower-class homes, regardless of race or ethnic origin, a naughty child is likely to be slapped or even punched. That is a fast punishment with few overtones except parental anger. It creates less guilt feelings than the more subtle mental penalties used by middle-class parents, which have other emotional overtones. However, the repeated use of rulers, belts, or straps to hit children for trivial classroom offenses, for lateness or truancy, for fighting, and even for failure to bring books and homework is brutalizing to both the child and the teacher or other school person charged with disciplinary responsibility. Brutality at home does not justify brutality in school. Moreover, such punishments inflicted over and over again on the same children for the same offenses fail to produce the desired behavior changes.

In all events, you must avoid becoming a punitive person. If you suspect that you punish too often, you may need to look within yourself to discover what your own childhood experience was and perhaps what personal drives you are expressing. Be quite sure, also, that you do not act out your fear of children, especially of Negroes, by using them as targets for abuse. Sometimes a fearful person thinks, "I'll show them first, before they show me."

The form of punishment most frequently used in school seems to be detention. If this means that the child returns at 3:30 p.m. to face an angry teacher who says, "Now you sit there and don't move until the clock says 4:15," little good is accomplished and the end result may be to increase hostility on both sides. If on the other hand the teacher uses the time for a one-to-one encounter and a face-to-face conversation with the child, the end result will be greater mutual understanding. With understanding comes acceptance and, for the child, willingness to obey and conform in order to learn. After such a session a child can go home saying, "That teacher digs me and I'm going to try."

Some forms of punishment used in bygone years seem to persist, although they are totally unwise. One of them is to make a child write 50, 100, or even 500 times a sentence like, "I will not talk any more." (It would be terrible if it actually did accomplish that goal.) Another punishment is the assignment of a large number of arithmetic examples or a composition on good behavior or extra work in any subject area. The net effect of such tasks is dislike of the subjects involved. If the teacher uses arithmetic or composition as punishment after school, who can blame children for looking on them as punishments in school.

Teachers in integrated schools ask if they should "lean over backwards" and not see when Negro children misbehave. They want to know if they should judge the Negro pupils' work more leniently and close their ears to bad language. The answer is no! If correcting behavior is important for whites, so it is for Negroes. If jacking up white children who slump in their work is a way to increase their effort and attention, so it is for Negro children. If pressuring children to do their best, to strive to be better, to aspire to be excellent is necessary to increase the achievement of white pupils, so it is for Negro pupils. Negro parents and children are not satisfied with leniency or with being overlooked. They want equality of interest, of treatment, and of opportunity to learn in the mixed

33

school. Until there is no difference in the quality and quantity of what you do for white and Negro pupils (as well as for other minority group children), you will not have achieved integration in your classroom.

There are some schools, particularly in center-city slum areas, in which almost all the children do as they please. They talk out loud all the time; they walk around the room; they throw paper and chalk at each other; they eat when they feel like it; practically no one listens to the teacher or does what the teacher tells him to do. Those conditions can exist only when, from the principal to the custodian, all adults have abdicated; all are ignoring their responsibilities. The children in such a school have taken over the adult roles. They have won the battle for leadership and domination.

Psychiatrists[1] tell us that a child who succeeds in dominating the situation, who has assumed the adult role, is bound to suffer from anxiety created by his unreadiness for that role and his inability to maintain it. Therefore, his tendency to act impulsively increases. His behavior becomes more uncontrollable by himself and the teacher.

The proper action to be taken in such a school is full discussion of their problems by the faculty and the principal with the help of qualified consultants. Then the faculty must formulate plans for change to which all agree and which all implement 100 percent at once.

Of course, parents have to be made part of the drive to make the school a proper place for learning. This means interpretation to PTA meetings, in-school conferences with individual parents, and home visits. Parents' aid and cooperation will have to be enlisted. When other methods are unsuccessful in "taming" individual students, drastic measures must be used until everyone knows what limits to behavior have been established for the entire school and that principal and teachers intend to enforce them.

Try to remember that a direct order may challenge a rebellious child to defy you. You have to know what you are prepared to do if he says, "No! I won't!" If possible, give him alternatives and their consequences, or remind him of the limits to behavior which he has violated and of the consequences which he helped to decide. Rebellion against adults, which is part of growing up, occurs more frequently as children move into adolescence.

---

[1]Stazvsky, W. H. "Using the Insights of Psychotherapy in Teaching." *Elementary School Journal* 58:28-35; October 1957.

How can I make them learn?

One of the greatest hazards for Negro children in a desegre-gated school is competition with white age-mates. From earliest childhood they have been made to believe that they are not as good as white people. They know that their adults, no matter how well qualified, have been rejected when they applied for work. They are aware of the uprisings that occur when a Negro family moves into a white neighborhood. They know their families cannot buy houses they want and can pay for in a middle-class neighborhood. They have had little or no chance to try and so are often convinced that they cannot win in competition with white age-mates. Furthermore, research has shown that in such competition, Negroes actually often do less than their best for fear of causing or increasing hostility in white teachers and classmates.

In the earlier discussion of acceptance you got some ideas for helping children to see themselves as likable people. When a child finds that others like him, he begins to like himself. However, you may have a hard time convincing a child that he is worthy of affec-tion if his father constantly tells him he is mean or that he is a devil. But once he is sure you like him, he can like you as well as himself and other people. An accepted child loses the anxiety that comes from rejection, and his energies are released for learning.

Self-worth also involves a sense of adequacy without which there can be little motivation or effort to learn. Adequacy comes from success, so it is of greatest importance to make sure that Negro children as well as the other children have some success experi-ences every day. Because all children do not learn easily from word symbols, you will have to use vicarious and direct learning ex-periences such as things, people, pictures, trips, radio, TV, films, dramatics, making things and taking them apart, and firsthand examination of the earth and all it possesses. This does not mean that you "throw the books out the window." But books and other printed materials must be on a wide range of reading levels.

If every child is to learn, you will have to plan tasks that vary in difficulty and length, for there is no such thing as a homogeneous group. Meeting individual differences and taking a child from where he is will involve you and the children in some one-to-one relationships. Much individual learning also goes on in small group work. When you arrange for that, do not place all the Negro children in the same ability group. They, like the white ones, will vary from excellent to poor in their ability to read, spell, do math, sing, paint, and use tools. Children like to help each other. You will speed the integration process when you assign an able Negro child to help a slower white one and when an able Negro is given leadership responsibility in group work, and vice versa. The cast for a dramatic production should be selected after tryouts in which the class helps to decide who is best for each part.

The concept of success is broader than the marking system. It involves taking note of, recognizing, and rewarding whatever is right rather than marking what is wrong. A basic learning principle is, emphasize what is right and reward a successful effort as soon as possible. Thus, when you give a spelling or an arithmetic test, if out of ten words or examples a child has even one or two right, say so on his paper, praise him for learning them, and tell him you expect he will get more right the next day.

Success does not require that you give a child only easy work. He must learn to stretch himself, but what he strives for must be within reach. If you use words rather than symbols to evaluate work, you will be able to praise and encourage each child, urge each one to make more effort, and caution each one against being content with less than his best. Avoid comparing children with each other, especially when they are of different races. Rather, for each one, place your emphasis on his doing better than he did before. All children will take pleasure in learning as soon as they know *how to learn.* Joy should come from knowing and knowing how to learn more rather than from marks.

Even little children, however, need a reason for working at school tasks. From upper-elementary grades on, you may have a hard job convincing some Negro and Spanish-speaking children that learning is worthwhile. Stories and pictures of people like them who became great, the life histories of today's Negro and other minority group leaders in government, industry, and the professions will help the nonwhite pupils to develop feelings of racial

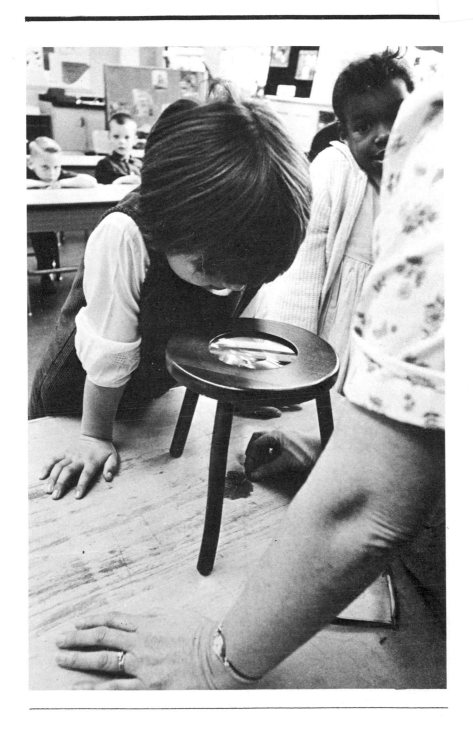

worth and the white ones to see that their feelings of racial superiority are unjustified. In secondary schools you can arrange for prominent minority group people in your community to address assemblies. Trips into the community to see mixed groups at work in business and industry and to interview Negroes and others in higher government positions and the professions are quite valuable learning experiences.

Feelings of worth come partly from identification with heroes and heroines in history, literature, and present-day life. The race, religion, and national origins of movie and TV stars, musicians, writers, artists, scientists, and sports champions should be identified, because children who use them as role models are often not aware of the racial, religious, and ethnic origins of the people they "worship."

Every human being throughout life has an ever present need to prove himself of ever greater worth. To satisfy that need, children's behavior sometimes takes strange and bizarre forms. Negro and other minority group children will not need to act up if they get assurance from you that as human beings they are good and therefore you like them; that they are able to learn and to become and therefore you respect them. When they know that their race makes no difference to you or to their classmates, you will have achieved integration in your classroom.

After a long period of years, a teacher found some notes in her "box of memories." They were laboriously printed, the teacher recalled, by a small Negro girl, who, until then, she hardly knew was there.

"Dear Miss Mary," the first one read, "I am sorry I have been bad all day. Plase forgive me. Thank you. I love you. Carale."

The second note, slipped into the teacher's hand the next day after she had at last *seen* the child, read, "Dear Miss Mary. I will try to work well in school. I will do my best. I will not be bad any more. I love you. Carol Ann Jones."

Do I need special kinds of learning materials?

Materials in a biracial classroom (as in all others) must appeal to children, for unless they enjoy the books, stories, pictures, and in kindergarten and first grade, the toys, they will reject them and not be able to learn from them. Children will not like the materials, however, unless they can identify with at least some of the people in the pictures and stories, can read about their own racial and ethnic groups in the history books, and can find out about problems which their own as well as the dominant groups are trying to solve. In most school systems, new and inexperienced teachers do not select books and equipment. In many, however, they and their colleagues do have some opportunities to make suggestions and to send in requests. The reasons why so-called multi-ethnic readers and supplementary materials are needed should be brought to the attention of all teachers.

Negro children are not the only ones who will benefit from more realistic materials. White children, too, must learn to live in a multicultured world in which positive attitudes toward racial difference are essential, for only one of every four people in the world is white. As adults, white people will increasingly work side by side with Negroes, be their employers and employees, be their pupils and their teachers, be their patients and their doctors, be their army officers and enlisted men fighting for freedom under their orders.

Be sure, then, that your bulletin board pictures all races. The family groups you show must be Negro as well as white. Work and play groups should show nonwhite and white people working and playing together. If you have dolls, be sure some have dark skin. Pictures of great people should include the great of all minority groups who have contributed to the development of all aspects of civilized life. Pictures of cities should include the depressed sections as well as the high-rise apartments and homes surrounded by lawns and gardens. When you select pictures, be sure to discard those which support negative stereotypes of Negroes doing only menial and semiskilled work, of Mexican-Americans as only migrant laborers, and of Indians as semicivilized idlers.

One of your objectives must be to create a new image of the Negro in his own mind as well as in the minds of white children and parents. Beautiful pictures of them can be found in such magazines as *Jet, Ebony,* and fashion magazines which picture Negro as well as white models. A number of publishers of basal reading series and picture books[1] have the kind of books you will need. If you are a secondary school teacher, current newspapers and news magazines will provide you with all you can use about race relations and problems of discrimination which the nation is trying to solve.

Pictures and play materials will help you to uncover prejudicial stereotypes and rejection of self in young children. Research tells us that Negro children at play prefer white dolls, think they are prettier, dress them in better clothes, and place them in better houses and in superior jobs. When interpreting pictures and telling stories or when older pupils write about pictures, Negroes often downgrade people like themselves. Suggestions for what you can do to build up self-esteem and eliminate prejudice are in several other sections of this book.

---

[1]Macmillan, Scott Foresman, Chandler, Ginn, John Day, and Judy Company of Minneapolis, are some of the publishers.

Why don't they participate?

Unless the Negro, Mexican-American, Puerto Rican, or Indian children are real eager beavers, they probably will wait to speak up or volunteer for tasks until you involve them in whatever is going on. A recitation period provides an opportunity to do so. However, some teachers still go up one row, down the next, calling on one child at a time in turn. If you do that, there is little likelihood that anyone other than the child called upon will listen to the questions until it comes near his turn to answer. Very often no one listens to the answer, which is directed to the teacher and is inaudible at any distance. Usually, teachers who conduct recitations that way repeat the answers in a loud voice hoping to catch the attention of the pupils. But repetition becomes boring and is a great waste of time.

If you want all the pupils to participate, ask your question, give the class a few moments to think of the answer, then call on someone. Don't repeat what he says, but involve another child by saying, for example, "Tim, is that your answer, too?" or "Sally, do you agree with what Morty said?" or "How many of you can add something to that answer?" Also, instead of saying "all right" to every answer (a bad habit which many teachers have), by your words, facial expression, tone of voice, and gestures, evaluate the answer and show your pleasure to each child who participates. Use such expressions as "Fine," "Good," "Excellent," "I like what you said," "Don't stop, we need to hear more from you," "Come in, we need your help," "You do have an idea (or suggestion) but it isn't quite what we need now," "Hold that (a not quite relevant answer) until later, but don't forget to tell us again." During such recitation periods, watch the faces, gestures, and postures, especially of your Negro or other minority group children, so that you can pick up

41

every clue that tells you when they are ready with some kind of contribution. If you call on them for answers and opinions, encourage them, and praise every effort they make, they will soon be an integral part of your group.

Discussions are different from recitations. The subject should be announced at least a day ahead and the students should be told where and how to get information about it. Children should not be involved in merely "exchanging ignorance" or in speculation without facts. Since all the pupils will not be reading at the same level, tell them that newspapers, magazines, pictures, and people are valid and respectable sources of information. Children need to develop the skills of learning from these sources as well as from text and reference books.

Make the furniture work for you to facilitate discussion. Placing chairs or desks in a circle is most helpful. If the group is too large for that, two-row circles can be used. Be sure, then, that the Negro (or other minority group) children are in the first row until they are well integrated. As often as possible pupils should see each other's faces rather than the backs of their heads and learn to talk across the circle to each other as well as to the teacher.

Until pupils have many experiences with discussion and you have had time to train some, you must be the leader. The process is not too different from that described for an effective recitation, except that you do not stimulate discussion by merely asking questions and you must avoid repeating and even commenting on everything pupils say. Be sure to keep an eye on the Negro children so that you can draw them into the conversation.

No matter what children say in discussion groups, there must be no shock or reprisal from you. Before talking begins, you and the class should set up some ground rules which will include no laughing at anyone unless he intends to be funny and giving every one the right to speak and be heard. Correction of English should be left for another time. Misstatements and factual errors must be noted, of course, but if correction can be delayed until other facts have been brought out, the child who made the mistake will suffer less from shame and hurt. All mistakes should be used as learning experiences and not be called failures.

Very often Negro or other minority children are unwilling to speak loudly enough to be heard or to volunteer answers, opinions, and comments because they are afraid of being wrong or of being laughed at or of being scolded for not knowing. Also, it takes some people a little longer to think and to get the words needed to express their thoughts. Teachers tend to pass over quickly the children they expect not to know and to give more time to those whom they expect to have the answers. Be sure you give every pupil whatever time he needs and receive with equal warmth and enthusiasm what each one has to say.

Sometimes children withdraw from participation because the subject under discussion or study has no connection with the reality of their lives. If it is just recall of factual textbook material, recitation is better than discussion. Social and moral issues and problems of living lend themselves to discussion.

Planning the day's program or the week's work or the unit should interest all the pupils if they know how to plan and if the teacher is sincere when he invites them to help in making decisions about what, when, and where to study and about who is to do what. Many children, both Negro and white, have little experience with the process and have rarely if ever, been admitted to decision making. Yet, if they are to behave effectively when they grow up, they must now develop skill in planning, in weighing facts for relative values, and in considering the consequences of alternative decisions. Pupil-teacher planning, especially in secondary schools, should be used for that purpose. The difficulty of involving the poor in planning community action programs in the current War on Poverty has pointed up their lack of skill in identifying common problems, setting up goals, planning actions for reaching those goals, accepting and fulfilling responsibilities, and evaluating themselves, the processes they use, and the final outcomes. Skill in any process depends upon opportunities for practice in meaningful situations. These should be provided to all children and youth in the public school.

Why not separate groups?

When children enter school at age five or six, they differ widely in the degree to which they have developed muscular coordination, vocabulary and the use of language, concepts of number relationships and of space and time, and readiness for learning to read. No matter how wide the differences, the children are put together in classroom groups.

Differences in growth and mental development do not disappear. They may, in fact, become more pronounced as the years go by. The teachers' problem from first grade on is how to meet these individual differences, how to arrange experiences so that every child learns. Mass instruction, which has long been used almost exclusively in many classrooms, will not accomplish the purpose; yet, many teachers have never experienced any other method of teaching and do not know how to diversify instruction.

For several decades, educators have tried grouping children on the basis of their mental abilities. Since reading is a tool needed for success in almost all subjects, scores on reading tests have been used as one criterion for determining to which groups pupils are to be assigned. However, because administrative necessity limits the number of groups, there are usually only three—top, middle, and bottom. In each of them, the range of the many abilities children have and need remains wide. Therefore, mass instruction still is not successful.

Whether or not grouping results in helping more children to learn depends upon many factors. Among these are how the teacher feels about the class to which he is assigned, his feelings about his own ability, and the skill with which he plans, instructs, and arranges many learning experiences.

45

Decisions about which child goes where are based not only on reading tests but also on IQ tests which are now known to produce far from valid measurements of any child's potentiality. They are particularly faulty in measuring the possible achievement levels that lower-socioeconomic-class children can reach. Placement decisions are based also upon teachers' subjective judgments registered as marks. These are heavily influenced by known or subconscious attitudes toward race, social class, and a teacher's projection of what a child might become.

Not all Negro or minority group children perform below grade level. Not all white children perform at or above grade level. Generalizations about ability to do academic work, based on race, are unwarranted and false when applied to individuals. To prejudge ability to succeed on the basis of race and on the expectation that Negroes will not be able to "keep up with the class" and therefore to automatically assign them to low ability groups is to do them a grave injustice. Considerable evidence indicates that ability grouping and tracking provide subtle but devastating outlets for acting out prejudices in the name of respectable educational techniques.

Ability grouping is especially hazardous, then, for Negro, lower-social-class whites, Spanish-speaking, and Indian children. It becomes a self-fulfilling prophecy for them and the teachers. When they are placed in low groups, the children realize that they are considered to be stupid and they tend to accept that judgment of their abilities. Their negative self-concepts are confirmed. Because they see themselves as slow or non-learners, they behave that way. Then teachers say, "I told you so; they are stupid."

Placement of Negroes and other minority group pupils in low-ability classes reinforces and supports the negative stereotypes that are currently held by many American public school people. A teacher who habitually thinks in stereotypes expects the so-called low-ability children to do poorly in academic subjects. His expectation determines how and what he prepares for them. Many a teacher, when assigned to those classes, says, "Well, I guess this year I'll have to just baby-sit," or "If I have to, I'll just try to entertain them." Baby-sitting and entertaining children are not enough.

The child who has no expectation of being successful in school, who has come to see himself as a symbol of failure, whose first reaction to a task is to say, "I can't," behaves as he perceives himself to be. He doesn't even try; he doesn't learn.

An exceptionally successful method of individualizing instruction is the use of able students to assist classmates in a one-to-one relationship. Many children whose minds work more slowly find it

46

easier to learn from another child. The bright, fast learners, when allowed to help classmates, experience the joy of sharing their talents and in the process consolidate their own learnings. (No one knows anything so well as when he has to teach it.)

Another method of sharing labor and individualizing assignments is small group work within the class. Teachers find this practically impossible unless they have some academically able pupils who can lead "research" committees, who can write well enough and have good enough judgment of the relative worth of facts to be recorders or secretaries, who can think fast enough to be leaders of discussion and conversation groups.

The effect of expectation connected with grouping, on how a child reacts, was well illustrated during an evening open house where a parent engaged a small boy in conversation. He asked the child a rather easy question and got the immediate response, "I don't know."

The man pressed the child, saying, "Come now, I'm sure you do. Why don't you know?"

Then the youngster mumbled, "I don't have to. I'm a turtle!"

The children in that school were divided into "hares" and "turtles." The teacher's constant spoken and implied feeling about him and his classmates had been, "Well, I guess I can't expect anything from you."

It would be difficult indeed to believe that children in low-ability classes have as equal an opportunity to learn and especially to learn from their peers as do pupils in mixed classes. The son of the editor of a large publishing house, who had been placed in a low group, said to him, "Dad, I'm not going back to school anymore. I just can't stand it. There is no one in the class that I can look up to."

Other evidence of inequality of opportunity was offered in a discussion group during an in-service education program. Teachers were exploring the use of dramatization and role playing as important devices for building self-confidence in slow learners. One teacher objected rather testily, saying, "But you couldn't let a Negro play the role of Little Red Riding Hood!"

"Certainly not," said another. "I wouldn't want to spoil that Nordic story!"

Equal educational opportunity means that every learning experience must be available to every child, regardless of race.

Lower-class pupils, both white and nonwhite, need to be in classes in which they can learn new ways of talking and behaving and new value patterns from middle-class white and nonwhite agemates. White children need the experience of both helping and

47

receiving help from Negro peers. Children of both races need to value each other so that as adults they will be able to live and work effectively in the democratic way and in a multiracial world.

Among the most harmful results of ability grouping and track systems are the emotional effects they have upon teachers. For example, slow progress causes boredom, which creates anxiety, feelings of guilt, and fatigue. Moreover, when children learn too slowly or when it seems to the teacher that they are not learning at all, he may become doubtful of his ability to teach. Then his negative self-concept reacts upon the quality of his classroom performance and that in turn reinforces his feeling of inferiority.

Politics and personal favoritism unfortunately play a part in determining which teacher gets which groups, especially the top ones. Another personal problem may enter the picture when a faculty includes Negro or Spanish-speaking teachers. They should not automatically be assigned to low-ability groups. It may be hard to convince some members of a faculty that the principal or his assistant, whoever makes the decisions, is not motivated by personal friendship or negative prejudice. Rarely does a teacher ask himself if he is more able than another to handle groups at the top or the bottom of the scale. Anger and jealousy over assignments to top groups often split up friendships, cause teachers to transfer, and prevent a faculty from having effective professional in-service education programs.

This presentation makes no pretense of giving anything other than the negative side of ability grouping. However, reports of success do come from situations in which teachers who know their own special qualifications volunteer to teach low-ability classes. Success in teaching middle and low groups (as well as heterogeneous groups) depends upon less use of mass instruction, more use of diversified methods and assignments, and the use of materials that have a wide range of reading levels. At the top level, students require quite different methods and materials. They should have full opportunity to become independent learners able to probe for and utilize facts gathered from many sources, including original sources, and to think deeply and critically about problems and issues. These same opportunities can and should be provided for able students in heterogeneous groups, plus the chance to work with all kinds of people.

Team teaching in heterogeneous groups is offering promise of success in individualizing instruction.

How can I make them all equal, at least in my room?

Equality of status is essential in the mixed classroom. Many white children are accustomed to thinking of the Negro as the low man on the totem pole, doing only menial work, the Indian as a savage, and the Mexican-American as a farmhand. They do not know that there are Negro (and other minority group) doctors, lawyers, writers, and scientists.

One day a mother, knowing that her child's first-grade teacher was Negro, asked, "Do you like your teacher?"

The child replied, "I haven't met my teacher. Every day she sends her maid."

Negro children are especially aware of the low status to which their race has heretofore been assigned in our society. They, like their white classmates, may be in a mixed situation for the first time. In fact, very often, going to the public school is the first experience children have of being with people different from themselves. In the mixed classroom, the teacher, no matter to what race or culture group he belongs, must play a neutral role as he strives to create *equality of status* for all the pupils.

Your children will know they have equality of status in your room when you treat them all with equal friendliness, kindness, and fairness; when you smile at them all with equal sincerity; when you praise with equal warmth; when you distribute chores and privileges impartially. In your classroom, Negro pupils must not become pets or mascots or scapegoats. Status established by you is likely to be accepted by children. If you find a child being unequally treated by his classmates, you must find the reasons and help him and them to alter whatever can be changed. Remember that skin color cannot be changed, and if that is the reason for the unequal treatment, you must attack the prejudices even little children possess.

Children feel very good about such personal attention, as for example, recognition of their birthdays. So, be sure your racial minority group pupils get cards from you if you send them to white children. In many poverty-stricken families birthdays are ignored and the children do not know what a party means. In one school, the teachers said the children did not know the word *refreshments*. Moreover, their mothers may not be able to send a cake or cookies or to provide popsicles for a class party. One way to handle this, if you have parties, is to arrange one a month for all who have birthdays during that month. Also, you protect those who cannot afford to contribute by making sure that no one knows who sends what refreshments each month.

If you make home visits, alternate white and Negro or other minority group families. If you visit sick children in hospital or at home or send them get-well cards or call on the phone to inquire about them, never omit doing so for your Negro, Mexican-American, Appalachian, and Indian pupils.

Housekeeping tasks, which children love to do, should be alternated. These include dusting board erasers, cleaning chalkboards, distributing and keeping track of books and other supplies, taking care of windows and curtains. It also includes taking messages to the office and to other teachers and acting as corridor monitors and hosts stationed in the office or front entrance to receive and direct visitors.

When leaders for teams and committees are needed, be sure Negro (and other minority group) pupils have their chance to fill such status positions. To do so you may need to appoint leaders until you are fairly sure that prejudice because of race or ethnic origin will not lead to rejection of children able to serve. Even then, a secret ballot for selection of leaders will be safer than a showing of hands. Choosing sides for team games is also a time when children suffer. It may be a quite terrible experience to wait and wait to be the last one named.

You will establish equality of status in your room when your words and deeds match your belief in the fullness of the worth of every individual. That in itself will also alleviate anxieties and thus release the energy needed for learning.

What shall we do about activities?

White teachers, especially in secondary schools, and parents in some white families are worried about the social implications of integration. They want to know, for example, about dancing. They know that in square dancing children may be asked to hold hands. They also think that in social dances Negro boys will ask white girls (or vice versa) to dance with them. Underneath is the fear that increased socializing is bound to lead to intermarriage. Studies of integration in housing and education fail to show that they do increase intermarriage.

Racial mixture has long been a fact in our society. All but a small percentage of Negro Americans carry white genes, because they have white as well as Negro ancestors. During slavery and thereafter in the South, Negroes were not the ones who initiated interracial unions. Moreover, in all probability, more children of mixed parentage are born in the South today, although that is where segregation is still most strictly enforced.

Studies of the social activities in integrated secondary schools show that mixed dancing or dating is not frequent, and when it does occur, it is usually initiated by white girls. But it certainly cannot be regarded as necessarily a prelude to marriage. It may be only an adolescent's desire to "kick over the traces" or defy parents and teachers who seem to the teen-agers to be prejudiced. Observers in schools desegregated for a long time usually remark how little mixing occurs in the lunchroom and that there are no mixed couples on the dance floor.

If a number of children in an elementary school class should voice their objections to holding a partner's hand in a game or square dance, it would be well to postpone those activities until the children, having seen that you have no such inhibitions and negative feelings, are ready to follow your lead. If only one child objects,

51

it is wise to go on with the activity but allow that child to be an onlooker until he is ready to join in the fun.

Teachers are influenced by each other and by their principals. On one occasion, in a school in which the faculty was being integrated, a Negro secretary was to be added to the office staff. When the principal informed the other secretaries of the fact, one of them, with tears in her eyes, said, "You don't expect me to go to lunch with her, do you?"

The principal answered, "No, I will, and when you are ready you may join us." It did not take long for her to do so.

People who promote desegregation in education do not intend to deny either teachers or children their right to personal preference and voluntary association. However, in schools where faculty desegregation has taken place, professional relationships across race lines have led some teachers into new and exciting friendships. They say that for them life has been enriched and they have become better people and better teachers. Children in integrated classrooms, because they have the chance to meet across race lines, are more likely to lose negative attitudes which, if they persist, will hinder their preparation for effective living in our democratic society and in the world where white people are in the minority.

Integration requires opening all school activities to Negro and other minority group pupils as well as to the dominant white group. If any child has been barred from any activity for lack of money or because he belongs to any minority group, now is the time to evaluate those activities in terms of democratic values and principles.

Joining and holding office in the service clubs and student councils, which are considered status activities, must be possible for all students regardless of race, color, creed, ethnic origin, or social class. It is not usually difficult to convince the students that election to office should be based solely on qualifications. However, over-zealousness in showing their lack of prejudice sometimes leads children and teen-agers to elect a Negro or other minority group student who is not qualified. This may place on him a burden too heavy to bear or may even cause him the humiliation of resigning. You must intervene early enough to prevent such a disaster, but in doing so it may be difficult to avoid the charge of prejudice.

Children tend to make a mascot of a single minority group child. The mascot role, like its opposite, the scapegoat role, is dangerous for the child as well as for the group. Try not to let either of those roles fall to a nonwhite pupil in your classroom.

Do Negro and lower-class children have needs
I don't know about?

First of all, be sure you *see* your Negro children. The title of Ralph Ellison's book, *Invisible Man*,[1] points to the traditional failure of teachers (and others, of course) to actually perceive Negroes as people who have the same needs, the same range of intellectual capabilities, the same emotional drives as whites. Look at, not over, your pupils; look into, not past, their eyes; look as deeply as you can into their minds and hearts.

To guide your search for information and understanding, consider the following questions:

• Does the child have enough energy to last through the day and to furnish the power needed for mental activity? (Energy comes from food, is renewed in sleep, is diminished by illness, and is produced in the process of metabolism.)

• Does he have food enough, adequate in quality and variety? (Poor families have little meat, rely on starches and sweets. There often is not enough to go around.)

• Does he get enough rest? How many others sleep in his bed? In the same room? Is the home quiet sufficiently early? (TV and radio often blare until early morning hours. Some parents quarrel through the night. The sounds of brawling and sex often keep children awake.)

• How well is the child? Have his injuries (possibly skull fractures or cracks) been cared for? Is he anemic? Does he have headaches and stomach aches? What of his teeth and eyes and ears? (Medical attention is costly and too often inaccessible to the poor. The elderly sick, the incapacitated, and the mentally ill usually remain at home and cause children to worry.)

---

[1] New York: Random House, 1952. 439 pp.

• Could his apathy or lethargy or obesity be due to low metabolism? Does anyone know or has anyone bothered to find out? (The family may not know that clinics are available or what kind of service to ask for.)

• Is he ashamed of being a Negro, a Mexican, a Puerto Rican? Of being poor? Of his clothing? Of having nothing for lunch? (Some children carry empty lunch boxes to school every day.)

• Is he ashamed of an alcoholic mother? Of a father confined to prison? Of having no father at all? (You will need to know all the answers before you pay a home visit or even summon a parent to come to the school.)

• Is he depressed and hopeless about himself because he has been told in one way or another since the first grade that he cannot read or that he will never learn to do arithmetic or "this school is not the place for you," or because he is in the lowest group? (When put into the lowest classes, many pupils call themselves dumbbells or nuts, stay away more often, and do not take part in after-school activities.)

• Does he know how to take objective tests, especially those "IQ tests"? (He may not have had the puzzles and games to play with that include questions and answers and depend on speed of response.) Does he get tired during these tests and so not finish them? (Encouragement when a child slumps will provide new energy.)

• Is he afraid? (Entering any kind of competition requires some belief in one's ability to win. It also takes courage.) Is he afraid that his classmates will jeer at him if he loses or hate him if he wins? (Hostility is part of the process of competition.)

• Does he know how to follow directions when you read them at the beginning of a test? Are the directions too complicated? (You could go to him and repeat them or help him to get started. You could put some clues on the board.)

• Does he value work? (He may never have seen his father get up, get ready, and hurry off to work every morning and bring home his pay envelopes. His family may have been on relief for as many as three generations. In slavery his ancestors could not work for money to keep themselves or to prepare for the future of their children.)

• Does he constantly say or think, "I can't"? (One must have a sense of adequacy to even try. Repeated experiences of failure deprive a child of belief in his ability to learn. You can help him to replace "I can't" with "I can.")

- Does he know anything about the history of his own race? (You can teach the whole class that Negroes have helped the nation to win every war; that many great men and women of the past and present are Negro; that the nation is now awake to what slavery and discrimination have done to Negroes; that the Negro civil rights organizations, together with white organizations and the nation's most powerful leaders, are working hard to correct the wrongs done in the past.)

- Does he know what opportunities lie ahead for him, what doors are now open, what hopes he can have for the future? (You can call on people who know and who have succeeded to tell him. You can take him out to see and hear firsthand.)

- What does he aspire to become? (You can help him to assess his strengths and weaknesses in relation to his aspirations. You must keep the doors of hope open while he works at developing his potentialities.)

- Does he have talents you haven't discovered? (In addition to recognizing their skills in reading and arithmetic, you could provide time for children to dance, sing, play their musical instruments, display muscular strength, do tricks and magic, and show their skills in mimicry and comedy.)

- Does the work in your classroom make sense to him? Does it relate to the reality of his life? Does it present the truth about the problems of his people? (He may need to know about himself and the actuality of the present before he can put his mind on the distant in time and place. You can study about emotions—fear, anger, hatred, race prejudice, feelings of inferiority, hurt caused by rejection—in literature, discuss these emotions in class, and write about them from open-end questions.)

- Is he preoccupied with problems of his rights, and does he understand his responsibilities? (The nation is in the midst of a great civil rights movement. You can make room for talk and study about it in your current events lessons nearly every day.)

- Does he know how to learn? (Some children believe that they fail to learn because the "teacher is no good." They do not know that they are responsible for learning. Maybe your emphasis in planning the daily work has to be shifted from teaching to learning.)

- Does he have to do homework or classwork from a book he cannot read? (If you assign lessons in a single text at your grade level, you will doom some of your pupils to failure.)

55

• Does he have any place at home where he can keep his school books and supplies? Does he have any place he can do schoolwork —a table to write on, a quiet corner, a room of his own? Is there a time when his brothers and sisters are also doing homework and his parents are reading? Does anyone at home ever ask if he has homework or has done it? (If all that is missing, you can't scold or punish him when he comes in without it. Maybe you can't even assign homework. In many schools "after-school work" has replaced homework, and after-school study rooms, where volunteer college students help elementary and high school students, are available.)

• Is the child confused because what is OK at home is wrong in school? (This might include the use of four-letter words, bad grammar, fighting, eating when hungry, taking what you need, distrusting authority and the police. You, too, are an authority figure and may have to win his trust.)

Some years ago the late James S. Plant pointed out that in our culture everyone has two lifelong needs: (1) the need for *whoness* —to be recognized as a person, to be liked and, if fortunate, loved; (2) the need for *whatness*—to be admired, approved for what one can achieve. Those who have been denied whoness often turn to an obsessive striving for whatness, seeking status, power, or property for the whoness they have missed.

What is the relation between race and intelligence?

Biological Aspects of Race

Biologists, geneticists, and anthropologists assembled by UNESCO[1] from seventeen countries unanimously approved thirteen statements on the biological aspects of the race question. The following excerpts from the statements are especially relevant to the content of this book for teachers.

All men living today belong to a single species, Homo sapiens, and are derived from a common stock. There are differences of opinion regarding how and when different human groups diverged from this common stock.

Biological differences between human beings are due to differences in hereditary constitution and to the influence of the environment on this genetic potential. In most cases, those differences are due to the interaction of these two sets of factors.

There is great genetic diversity within all human populations. Pure races—in the sense of genetically homogeneous populations—do not exist in the human species.

There are obvious physical differences between populations living in different geographic areas of the world, in their average appearance. Many of these differences have a genetic component.

Most often the latter consist in differences in the frequency of the same hereditary characters.

Different classifications of mankind into major stocks, and of those into more restricted categories (races, which are groups of populations, or single populations) have been pro-

---

[1]The UNESCO Moscow Conference on Race included twenty-two biologists, geneticists, and anthropologists from seventeen countries.

posed on the basis of hereditary physical traits. Nearly all classifications recognize at least three major stocks. . . .

Many anthropologists, while stressing the importance of human variation, believe that the scientific interest of these classifications is limited, and even that they carry the risk of inviting abusive generalizations. . . .

Differences between individuals within a race or within a population are often greater than the average differences between races or populations.

Some of the variable distinctive traits which are generally chosen as criteria to characterize a race are either independently inherited or show only varying degrees of association between them within each population. Therefore, the combination of these traits in most individuals does not correspond to the typological racial characterization. . . .

Certain physical characters have a universal biological value for the survival of the human species, irrespective of the environment. The differences on which racial classifications are based do not affect these characters and, therefore, it is not possible from the biological point of view to speak in any way whatsoever of a general inferiority or superiority of this or that race.

Human evolution presents attributes of capital importance which are specific to the species.

The human species, which now spread over the whole world, has a past rich in migrations, in territorial expansions and contractions.

As a consequence, general adaptability to the most diverse environments is in man more pronounced than his adaptations to specific environments.

For long millennia, progress made by man, in any field, seems to have been increasingly, if not exclusively, based on culture and the transmission of cultural achievements and not on the transmission of genetic endowment. This implies a modification in the role of natural selection in man today. . . .

As a rule, the major stocks extend over vast territories encompassing many diverse populations which differ in language, economy, [and] culture. . . .

There is no national, religious, geographic, linguistic or cultural group which constitutes a race ipso facto; the concept of race is purely biological.

However, human beings who speak the same language and share the same culture have a tendency to intermarry, and often there is as a result a certain degree of coincidence between physical traits on the one hand, and linguistic and cultural traits on the other. But there is no known causal nexus between these and therefore it is not justifiable to attribute cultural characteristics to the influence of the genetic inheritance.

Most racial classifications of mankind do not include mental traits or attributes as a taxonomic criterion.

Heredity may have an influence in the variability shown by individuals within a given population in their responses to the psychological tests currently applied.

However, no difference has ever been detected convincingly in the hereditary endowments of human groups in regard to what is measured by these tests. On the other hand, ample evidence attests to the influence of physical, cultural and social environment on differences in response to these tests. . . .

The genetic capacity for intellectual development, like certain major anatomical traits peculiar to the species, is one of the biological traits essential for its survival in any natural or social environment.

The peoples of the world today appear to possess equal biological potentialities for attaining any civilizational level. Differences in the achievements of different peoples must be attributed solely to their cultural history.

Certain psychological traits are at times attributed to particular peoples. Whether or not such assertions are valid, we do not find any basis for ascribing such traits to hereditary factors, until proof to the contrary is given. Neither in the field of hereditary potentialities concerning the over-all intelligence and the capacity for cultural development, nor in that of physical traits, is there any justification for the concept of "inferior" and "superior" races.[2]

Mental Aspects of Race

A committee of social scientists, including psychologists and geneticists, assembled at a UNESCO conference in Paris, issued a joint statement which included the following statement on the relation between intelligence and ethnic origin:

Whatever classifications the anthropologist makes of man, he never includes mental characteristics as part of those classifications. It is now generally recognized that intelligence

---

[2]Excerpts from "Biological Aspects of the Race Question." *UNESCO Chronicle* 10:348-52; November 1964. Reproduced by permission of UNESCO.

tests do not themselves enable us to differentiate safely between what is due to innate capacity and what is the result of environmental influences, training and education. Wherever it has been possible to make all allowances for differences in environmental opportunities, the tests have shown essential similarity in mental characters among all human groups. In short, given similar degrees of cultural opportunity to realize their potentialities, the average achievement of the members of each ethnic group is about the same.

For several years a few people have challenged the scientists who have been working on the relationship of race to intelligence. In an effort to refute their attempts to prove that the Negro is natively inferior in intelligence to the white, Dr. Melvin M. Tumin, Princeton University sociologist, questioned four outstanding authorities on testing, psychology, sociology, and anthropology about those contentions. Summarizing their replies, Dr. Tumin writes:

> *The four scientists are in substantial agreement that the claims . . . [of racial intellectual inferiority] cannot be supported by any substantial scientific evidence.*
>
> *Moreover . . . any future claims regarding innate differences between Negroes and whites with regard to intelligence cannot be substantiated unless three conditions are met:*
>
> *(1) The distinctive genetic, or "racial," homogeneity of the Negro group being tested, as well as that of the white group being tested, must be demonstrated, not assumed.*
>
> *(2) The social and cultural backgrounds of the Negroes and whites being tested or otherwise being measured must be fully equal.*
>
> *(3) Adequate tests of native intelligence and other mental and psychological capacities, with proven reliability and validity, will have to be used.*
>
> *To date, none of these crucial conditions has been satisfactorily met.[3]*

In a statement on racial imbalance in public schools, Dr. Thomas F. Pettigrew and Dr. Patricia J. Paponas, Harvard University social psychologists, at a New York State Education Department conference, March 31, 1964, described how nonwhites in American society act out the Negro role of socially defined inferior. They said that many white people confuse that *role* with the *per-*

---

[3]Tumin, Melvin M. *Race and Intelligence: A Scientific Evaluation.* New York: Anti-Defamation League of B'nai B'rith, 1963. 56 pp.

sons who play it. Thus, the stereotyped traits of laziness, uncon-
cern, and stupidity are assumed to be characteristics which all
Negroes possess. They indicate that the child, as he plays up to the
expectation of not being bright, assumes "a facade of stupidity as
a defense mechanism . . . is not eager to learn, [does] not strive to
do well in intelligence testing situations." Thus, the common belief
that the two races differ in intelligence *seems* to be confirmed by
the lower IQ scores generally made by Negro children as compared
to whites of similar ages.

An extensive and definitive survey of what research has revealed about the intelligence of Negro Americans is reported in
"Negro American Intelligence: A New Look at an Old Contro-
versy," by Thomas F. Pettigrew, which appeared in the *Journal of
Negro Education*[4] and was later expanded and fully documented in
his book, *Profile of the Negro American.*[5] Of particular importance
to teachers are the research studies he cites to refute the charges
made by a few writers that there is scientific evidence to prove that,
as a race, Negro Americans have inferior intelligence. The few of
the 565 references which document Dr. Pettigrew's book which are
listed below were selected for their relevance to the content of
this publication. All quoted statements are from Dr. Pettigrew's
writings.

Anastasi, Anne. "Intelligence and Family Size." *Psychological Bulletin* 53: 187-209; May 1956.

Canady, H. G. "The Effect of 'Rapport' on the IQ: A New Approach
to the Problem of Racial Psychology." *Journal of Negro Education*
5: 209-19; April 1936.

Cooper, R. M., and Zubeck, J. M. "Effects of Enriched and Con-
stricted Early Environments on the Learning Ability of Bright and
Dull Rats." *Canadian Journal of Psychology* 12: 159-64; 1958.

Deutsch, Martin. "Minority Group and Class Status as Related to
Social and Personality Factors in Scholastic Achievement." *Mono-
graph of the Society for Applied Anthropology* 1-32; No. 2, 1960.

Deutsch, Martin, and Brown, B. "Social Influences in Negro-White
Intelligence Differences." *Journal of Social Issues* 20: No. 2, 1964.

Haggard, E. A. "Social Status and Intelligence: An Experimental
Study of Certain Cultural Determinants of Measured Intelligence."
Genetic Psychology Monographs 49: 141-86; 1954.

[4]33: 6-25; Winter 1964
[5]Copyright 1964, D. Van Nostrand Company, Inc., Princeton, N.J.

Hunt, J. M. *Intelligence and Experience*. New York: Ronald Press, 1951.

Knoblock, Hilda, and Pasamanick, B. "The Contribution of Some Organic Factors to School Retardation in Negro Children." *Journal of Negro Education* 27: 4-9; Winter 1958.

Lee, E. S. "Negro Intelligence and Selective Migration: A Philadelphia Test of the Klineberg Hypothesis." *American Sociological Review* 16: 227-33; 1951.

Pasamanick, B., and Knoblock, Hilda. "Early Language Behavior in Negro Children and the Testing of Intelligence." *Journal of Abnormal and Social Psychology* 50: 401-402; No. 3, May 1955.

Piaget, J. *The Psychology of Intelligence*. London: Routledge and Kegan Paul, 1947.

Trumbull, R. "A Study in Relationships Between Factors of Personality and Intelligence." *Journal of Social Psychology* 38: 161-73; November 1953.

There is no room left to doubt that intelligence is not a fixed entity determined by the individual's genes long before his birth. Piaget provides "abundant evidence that intelligence is the very antithesis of a fixed, predetermined capacity."[6] Psychologists have already described more than fifty elements that constitute the complex potentialities, achieved mental abilities, and developed characteristics by which the classroom teacher judges a child to be below average, average, or superior. Psychologists and other scientists are now asserting that what "intelligence" the child manifests may be merely what he has thus far developed and, of utmost importance, are saying that "intelligence can be created."

The research upon which Dr. Pettigrew draws in his book clarifies the factors that operate to block development of intelligence and what factors must be present in a child's life for intelligence to grow. He calls the former "mediators of intellectual underdevelopment." These include, for example, lack of iron and vitamin B complex during the mother's pregnancy, premature birth, and brain injury.

Of particular importance to teachers are research studies which indicate that inferior schooling, in fact the very nature of the public schools which so many lower-socioeconomic-class Negroes have attended, are the causes of noticeable decreases in IQ scores as some of them get older. Pettigrew recalls that in "one

---

[6]*Ibid.*, p. 108.

. . . study of 'verbal destitution' those Negro students most retarded in a reading clinic came from small, segregated high schools and exhibited language patterns typical of the only adult models they had encountered—poorly educated parents, teachers, and ministers."[7]

Other blocks to development of intelligence exist when families are disrupted. The absence of a father and employment of both parents reduce the children's contacts with adults who ordinarily teach them most of what they know up to the age of six when they enroll in school. It is common knowledge that more Negro families than white are not only disorganized but large. When there are many children to be cared for, parental contact is necessarily thinly spread.

One factor which has serious effects on development of intelligence is the negative self-image which carries with it belief that the self is inferior. Educators are assured by psychiatrists that the individual behaves as he perceives himself to be. This belief in his inferiority depresses achievements in test taking and in other school situations in which a Negro is in competition with whites. Moreover, lack of self-confidence and fear of increasing hostility by being superior create anxiety which interferes with performance. Dr. Pettigrew says that "achieving a high test score does not have the same meaning for a lower-status Negro child [as it does for a white middle-class child], and it may even carry a definite connotation of personal threat . . . scoring low may for some talented Negro children be a rational response to perceived danger."[8]

Deprivation of experiences with things, toys, games, automatic devices, pictures, nursery rhymes, fairy stories, all the manifestations of nature, and most of all with people constitutes the greatest of all blocks to development of intelligence. It is through a rich environment, a multiplicity of experiences, help in understanding relationships and in learning to use language that intelligence is created. Much attention is now being given to providing all of these at an early age for economically deprived children.

To quote Dr. Pettigrew once more, "Intelligence . . . is a dynamic on-going set of processes that within wide hereditary limits is subject to innumerable experiential factors."[9] The "deprived environments" which have been shown to have "intellectually damaging consequences"[10] are characteristic of the slums and depressed

[7]Ibid., p. 112.
[8]Ibid., p. 115.
[9]Ibid., p. 107.
[10]Ibid., p. 110.

areas of many urban and rural communities in which lower-social-class Negro, Mexican-American, Puerto Rican, and mountain people live. To ascribe to lack of intelligence their unreadiness for schooling, their slowness in learning to read (especially bilingual children), and the difficulty they have in expressing their thoughts is to be uninformed about the facts and manifestly unjust.

Many studies show that when individuals in any group move from a restrictive to a stimulating environment, their measured IQs rise. Thus far, the experience with desegregation indicates that this does happen to Negro children when they are placed in classrooms with middle-class children and have teachers who perceive themselves to be responsible for the fullest possible development of every child's unknown potentiality.

Isn't there much talent going to waste?

Our Wasted Potential[1]
by Daniel C. Thompson
Professor of Sociology
Dillard University, New Orleans, Louisiana

Ours is an awe-inspiring age. We contemplate the future of mankind generally, and the future of our own society specifically, with mingled optimism and fear. On the one hand, man's eternal desire to build a better world, to reconstruct society in such a way that ignorance, poverty, diseases, inequalities, fears and wars will either be eliminated or greatly reduced, offers—at long last—some real hope of fulfillment. On the other hand, our capability for destruction, for actually wiping out civilization as we know it, is infinitely greater, and even more disquietingly probable, than at any other time in history.

. . . In the final analysis, whether mankind proceeds in the direction of creative social reconstruction or international destruction, whether our own nation continues to grow stronger and more significant as the leader of the free world, or declines in strength and ceases to be a symbol of freedom and democracy will be determined in very large part, not just by our economic and military strength, but the degree to which we find ways of developing our most basic resource—our human potential. Pointedly, the true greatness of this nation, or any nation, will be determined in the future (even now) by the level of its education, skills, scientific know-how, morale and the general character of the citizens, as well as by its military strength.

. . . Arnold J. Toynbee, the noted British scholar, concluded after a long and exhaustive analysis of world history, that practically all of the fallen civilizations of the past—such as ancient

[1]From Klopf, Gordon J., and Laster, Israel A., eds. *Integrating the Urban School.* Proceedings of the Conference on Integration in the New York City Public Schools. New York: Bureau of Publications, Teachers College, Columbia University, 1963. pp. 1-11. Reproduced by permission of the author and the publisher.

Egypt, Rome, Babylon, Greece, and Syria—began to decline, and most of them actually fell during their most economically prosperous period, when their armies were larger and better equipped than ever before in their nation's history. Why, then, did these great civilizations decline, fall and finally disappear as such? Toynbee suggests the answer: These great nations allowed their youth to become defiled—or they failed to pass on to their youth the high ideals, the basic values, the fundamental skills, and the nobility of purpose which, in the first place, brought their nations to greatness. Thus the lesson of history is this: Our nation will begin to decline in strength and nobility of purpose, and could eventually fall, unless we take care to conserve and develop our most precious, and altogether indispensable, resource—*the youth of this nation.*

On this point President John F. Kennedy . . . [said]:

Our progress as a nation can be no swifter than our progress in education. Our requirements for world leadership, our hopes for economic growth, and the demands of citizenship itself in an era such as this all require the maximum development of every young American's capacity. The human mind is our fundamental resource.

With this warning in mind we should become fully aware that the wide gap between the academic achievements of certain culturally deprived groups in our cities, particularly Negro youth and the average American child, is a national problem of the first magnitude. It indicates a tragic waste of talents and abilities which we simply cannot afford because our national greatness and international leadership depend ultimately upon the general quality of our population, upon the developed potential of each individual citizen.

We are already beginning to see how unwise it is to allow the great potential among our Negro youth to lie fallow, undeveloped, and unused. In practically every large city in the United States— especially in the large Northern metropolises such as New York —problems stemming from widespread frustration and social disorganization on the part of Negroes are threatening not only to destroy the hopes as well as the talents of the masses of Negroes, themselves, but the very economic, social, and moral foundation of our society.

Symptoms of this gradual but steady decay in the system of values that undergirds American society are now so obvious that they can no longer be ignored or discounted. Among the most easily recognized symptoms are the steadily increasing rate of delinquency, crime, illegitimacy, dropouts, unemployment, and general unrest among our youth. As high as these rates are among Americans on the whole, they are up to five times as high among Negroes.

The Problem

In order to get a functional understanding of the nature and extent of the wasted talents among Negro youth it is necessary, first of all, to take into account three basic social facts:

(1) All human behavior is fundamentally normal behavior in the sense that it is learned. This is so whether a given pattern of behavior is regarded as socially reprehensible or socially approved. The basic motivations to learn or participate in a given pattern of behavior are the desire for security, the desire for recognition, the desire for new experience, and the desire for response.[2] Therefore, what is regarded generally as socially deviant behavior is basically a reflection of defects in education, or more broadly, in the process of socialization, whereby the child has not been brought to accept certain important norms and values which prevail in society as a whole; or he has come to internalize certain antisocial norms and values peculiar to some given social world or class of which he is a part. In other words, the child will tend to use the rules, techniques, and methods accepted by his reference group (a group or social world to which he either belongs or desires to belong) in his attempts to satisfy the basic desires just mentioned.

(2) No matter how social class may be defined—whether in terms of wealth, education, style of life, occupation, or aspiration— approximately 70 to 80 percent of the Negro population in large Northern cities are lower class.

Generally speaking, lower-class parents are far too busy with the exigencies of day-to-day living to give much creative thought to long-range planning for their children. Thus during the past few years I have done several studies that revealed the vast wasted potential among Negro youth, particularly boys.[3] The following are characteristics of the Negro homes from which come the great majority of dropouts, delinquents, and unemployed youth:

---

[2]Thomas, W. I. *The Unadjusted Girl*. Boston: Little, Brown and Co., 1928. pp. 1-40.

[3]Thompson, Daniel C. "A Profile of Social Classes in the Negro Community," *Proceedings of the Louisiana Academy of Sciences* (1956); *The Eighth Generation*, New York: Harper and Bros., 1960; "The Changing Status of Negroes in New Orleans," *The Journal of Social Science Teachers*, May 1957; "The Social History of a Religious Cult," M.A. thesis; "Social Class Factors in Public School Education as Related to Desegregation," *American Journal of Orthopsychiatry*, July 1956; "The Formation of Social Attitudes," *American Journal of Orthopsychiatry*, January 1962.

(a) In about half of the homes one or both parents had a history of alcoholism, criminality, poverty, and instability.

(b) Practically all of the homes may be described as *culturally impoverished*. As a rule neither parent (or guardian) had received as much as a high school education. Furthermore, there was seldom any reading material found in their homes except the elementary school books used by the children.

In most homes there was a television or radio set, and sometimes a record player, yet members of the family had no manifest interest in any form of music and drama except that which might be classified as "low brow." Seldom did any member of the family listen attentively to news broadcasts or other types of informational programs.

(c) The houses, like the neighborhoods, in which they lived were generally ugly. There was seldom any effort to make surroundings beautiful with flowers, pictures or furnishings, and there were very few homes that had a spare room where the children could study quietly.

(d) About a fourth of the children were born out of wedlock. Some parents were quick to admit that their children were unwanted.

(e) There was little evidence of family pride.

(f) Half of the homes were without a male head. Even when the father was present, the mother appeared to be the dominant figure.

(g) Parents had made no definite plans for their children's future. None, for example, had education policies to insure their children's schooling.

(h) By and large parents did not teach their children self-respect. More often the child was depreciated and derogated.

(i) Children had not been taught to aspire for more than day-to-day success. For instance, only occasionally did a dropout or delinquent express any future occupational aspiration at all. When pressed to state some occupational aspiration they would casually name some "low-aspiration" occupation.

(j) The "problem" children had no clear conception of success as defined in traditional American thought. None identified with a great legendary or real hero in history. Actually the parents had never told these children traditional bedtime stories which function to delineate acceptable heroes or heroines.

(k) Case histories of most of these families revealed a series of traumatic stresses, strains and breakups brought on by chronic illness, imprisonment, poverty and/or separations.

(1) There was ample validation of the fact of the old proverb: "The apple does not fall far from the tree." That is, the several studies underscored the fact that children are not often very different from their parents.

Finally among lower-class Negroes there are at least four distinct social worlds: (1) the matriarchy, where the fact of being *female* is given great emphasis and *maleness* is a symbol of distrust, disrespect, and dishonor; (2) the gang, where *maleness* is defined in terms of aggressiveness, physical prowess, and the necessity to "prove yourself a man." Boys from matriarchal homes learn early to disrespect women—actually to reject any value associated with femaleness. Thus from the very start two large segments of Negro mass society are set against one another: Girls born and reared in matriarchal homes tend to distrust men and reject values identified with the "male principle" in society. Boys find various ways to demonstrate their rejection of the "female principle." In a sense, then, girls and boys reared in matriarchal homes become "natural enemies." This fact is basic in mapping out an approach to effective education. (3) Marginality, where children have shifted from one place to another, from one family to another, and from one self-identity to another so often they have not had time to develop a stable self-identity. This confusion is reflected whenever they must make any decision, including school, courtship, or employment. (4) The nuclear family, where family members are tightly banded together, as it were, for protection against the outside world. Children from these homes tend to be suspicious, even of those who try to help them. In a sense, however, it is one of the most wholesome social worlds for the psychological development of children because there is considerable family pride, stability, and more or less, clear self-identity.

Any program of compensatory education must take into account the fact that lower-class Negro children suffer from different kinds of deprivations. Some need to develop wholesome attitudes regarding sex statuses and roles, some need to achieve stable self-identities, and others need to be taught that the world can be friendly, not just hostile. Most need to be made to feel that they are accepted as worthy participants in the middle-class-oriented schools to which they may be assigned.

(3) A third basic fact to be considered is that social structure in white society is the reverse of that in Negro society. That is, from 70 to 80 percent of the white urban population may be classified as middle and upper class. This means that American culture generally, and schools in particular, are middle-class oriented. They

lay great emphasis upon such values as self-respect, achieved social status and recognition, higher education, occupational success, stable family life, the willingness to sacrifice the satisfaction of immediate desires for long-range goals, hard work, and morality.

Now, let us again define our basic problem. It seems to be this: *How can we successfully and effectively integrate socially, culturally, and psychologically deprived Negro children into the best schools of our nation so that they might be prepared to participate in the mainstream of our American culture?*

. . . .

Rural Cultural Background

At the close of the Civil War about 90 percent of the Negroes lived in the rural South. Today this has changed—about 40 percent, or eight million or so, live outside the South. Thus, for instance, during the last two decades the Negro population in New York City has increased nearly two and a half times, and now numbers over a million and constitutes at least fourteen percent of the total population. Furthermore, a steady stream of Negro migrants is still flowing out of the South to this and other cities of the North and West.

At the close of World War II the danger of the wide educational gap between the masses of Negro children and the average white child became glaringly apparent. A few of this nation's leaders more or less mildly suggested that we could hardly afford to continue to waste the great potential in the Negro race as had been done over the years. Eventually Congress was asked to appropriate federal money to equalize educational opportunities throughout the nation. Ironically, the very states that would have benefitted most from such a program (the Southern states) led the vicious fight to defeat this proposal because it would have included their Negro citizens. Many shortsighted Northern congressmen could always be depended upon to join with their Southern colleagues in defeating any attempt to equalize educational opportunities in the Southern states. Therefore, gross inequalities in the educational opportunities for Negro youth in the South were allowed to remain.

The Negro Ghetto

Frustrated and discouraged Negroes left Southern communities in search of better conditions, including better education for their children. For the most part they settled in segregated Northern slums. Steadily these slums became bigger and bigger and more withdrawn from the mainstream of the city's culture and what was once a Southern problem has now become the problem of New York . . . [and other large cities].

Gradually the Negro ghetto became increasingly like some of the culturally deprived communities from which the Negroes had migrated. The schools they found in Northern cities were, in some respects, very much better than the ones they left but not nearly good enough to equip them for the greater competition they encountered in these cities.

Some parents became completely dissatisfied and demanded the right to send their children to the higher standard schools attended by white children. Thus in 1958, in the Skipworth case, the

Court agreed that Negro parents were [within] . . . their rights to insist that their children should attend the best public schools available. Therefore, New York [and other large cities] can no longer contain the problem of Negro education in a given area of the city. *It is no longer the problem of educating Harlem [or slum] Negroes —but culturally deprived New Yorkers [city dwellers] of all races.*

How the Problem of Cultural Deprivation Might Be Solved

Many New Yorkers [for example] described the Negro youngsters who transferred to formerly all white, or predominantly white, schools as "invaders." They seemed unable to comprehend that a child born in the rural areas of Mississippi is an American with the same rights as other Americans—that he has as much right to attend any school in New York City as does a child born in the most economically advantaged communities of this city. Therefore, the wiser New Yorkers did not define these Negro children as invaders —but as a "problem." Consequently, some noteworthy attempts have been made to bridge, or close, the scholastic gap between the culturally deprived and the more culturally fortunate in the schools [of most cities]. . . . [However] the problem is very far from being solved.

There are at least three possible approaches to the desegregation of schools:

(1) *The track program.* According to this program children are divided into three groups in terms of achievement. Those in the highest track are prepared for higher education, those in the middle track for certain white-collar and skilled pursuits where average talents are needed, and those in the lowest track are encouraged to prepare for certain manual jobs.

Though refusing to take a stand on the merit of the track system. Conant[1] does say: "I submit that in a heavily urbanized and industrialized free society the educational experiences of youth should fit their subsequent employment."

There are at least two fallacies in this reasoning: One, experience has proven that it is extremely dangerous (even when we use the most advanced tests) to predict the future capabilities of a child ten or twelve years of age. With expert training some children whose IQ's were apparently well below average, and whose motivation was very weak, showed great improvements in both and proved to be capable of qualifying for almost any occupation in our society.

---

[1]Conant, James B. *Slums and Suburbs.* New York: McGraw-Hill Book Co., 1961. p. 40.

Two, to prepare a child for some specific occupation he is supposed to pursue twenty or thirty years in the future requires an impossible prognosis. In this rapidly changing technological society no one can say what old occupations will remain and what new occupations will be created.

(2) A second approach to desegregation is that of having what amounts to *three types of schools.* In this way the so-called "mentally superior" will be recruited from all segments of society just as will those of "average" and "below average" mentality, each group having its own specialized school.

Here again, an undemocratic decision must be made. It is true that a competent scientist or professor must have at least average mentality, yet the truth remains that society is not built by the mentally superior only, and there is in practically everyone hidden potential that may blossom with nurture. Furthermore, some of our most prolific "geniuses" have developed in the same schools with fellow students of just average abilities.

(3) *Democratic education.* The fundamental philosophy undergirding public school education in this country is that every American child should have the same educational opportunity as every other child. That is, in the competition for an education and for the rewards it may bring, *each individual child has the same right as every other child to succeed or fail.*

It may be that we are so scientifically advanced that we can save the child from needless academic failure. *I don't think so.* I don't think that we have had nearly enough experiments in democratic education to abandon it just yet. We need to continue to experiment in our efforts to make equal education available to all of our youth.

In order to provide the culturally deprived child with an equal democratic education I propose the following general approach:

(1) Our government on all levels (federal, state, and local) will need to appropriate considerably more money for education than is now being done. As I see it we will need to spend something like twice the proportion of our tax money for the education of the culturally deprived as we do for those who are culturally fortunate. Therefore, our school systems would need to adopt flexible policies regarding educational experimentation.

(2) Foundations would need to bear most of the cost of experimentation and research. They would need to concentrate much of their funds, also, in the training of teachers specialized in dealing with the culturally deprived. *The most promising way of closing*

73

the cultural gap between the lower-class Negro youth and the pre-dominantly middle-class white youth is superior teaching.

Negro colleges are peculiarly equipped to provide the quality of teachers needed for the compensatory education Negro migrant children need. If foundations would provide funds whereby two or three percent of the Negro and white college students could be carefully selected and intensely trained in these colleges under the personal supervision of professors who are, themselves, well trained in Negro history and culture, it would be possible to produce a large number of teachers who are able to provide culturally deprived children with the insightful guidance and instruction they must have in order to develop their potentialities.

These specially trained teachers could solve two critical personnel problems: the flight of good teachers from predominantly Negro schools, and the acute shortage of male teachers.

As I see it college juniors would be selected for this program. They would be provided full college expenses and an additional year of graduate training especially structured to prepare them for the teaching of the culturally deprived. When they qualify for the program they would be paid considerably higher salaries than other teachers and given special social recognition. (The differential pay would be justified on the basis of their superior training in a specialized area of education.)

(3) Total community involvement is needed. It is my belief that when the government and foundations attempt to shoulder the total burden of educational improvement, most of their effort will be wasted. There must be generated a community-wide concern. All organizations and individuals in the community should be drawn into the program of integration and cultural uplift. This means that such a program will be well thought out so that specific, detailed functions and tasks can be precisely assigned. When the individuals and organizations know precisely what is expected of them they can be expected to cooperate. Also they must be able to see exactly why their small or large contribution is essential to the success of the total operation. In this way hitherto untapped community resources can be channeled into an all-out educational program.

Finally, if we would save and develop the vast wasted talents and abilities among our culturally deprived youth, government on all levels, philanthropic foundations, talented individuals, and all organizations in the respective communities must pool their resources in a unified effort to bridge the cultural gap between these youth and others who have been socialized in superior middle-class homes and neighborhoods.

What is the meaning of skin color to Negro children?

"It's the Same, but It's Different" [1]
by Robert Coles, M.D.
Psychologist
Harvard University, Cambridge, Massachusetts

Sally, one of the Negro children I knew in . . . [a Southern city],
drew heavily upon her grandmother's spirit when confronted with
the hate and violence of mobs and the forced, pointed loneliness
brought on by the boycott of "her" desegregated school. The little
girl had been born . . . in her grandmother's farmhouse—unlike
many of those nearby, a rather solid building. Her grandparents
were, in fact, relatively prosperous and substantial people in their
community, having acquired title to their land, added to it, culti-
vated it wisely and assiduously, and eventually invested its profits
in a neighborhood store. *(Their* parents had been sharecroppers,
their grandparents, slaves.) Running the store was now the grandmother's business; her husband still cared for his farm, though with
considerable help from several of his sons. Sally's mother had
wanted to stay in that small town. It was her husband who took his
wife and two small children to . . . [the city]. He wanted a job of
his own, away from farm work and running errands at the family
store. Sally was four at the time, and disliked leaving her grandmother. Still, she saw her regularly, for her parents continued to
make weekend trips to the country.

Like the other three girls selected [for this study], Sally (and
her parents) had no idea that she would face exposure to mobs as
the price for entering a once all-white elementary school. Her parents had submitted her application because many of their neighbors
were doing likewise. Having arrived only recently in . . . [the city],
they had assumed that its attitudes were not those of the state's
rural areas. So much else was different . . . its buildings that anyone

[1]From *Daedalus* 94:1107-32; Fall 1965. Reproduced by permission of the
author and the publisher, the American Academy of Arts and Sciences, Boston,
Massachusetts.

could enter, its streetcars where anyone could sit anywhere, its sidewalks where Negroes could walk on the "inside" without interruption instead of retiring to the road at the approach of a white person, its stores serving *all* customers by proper turn—that school desegregation seemed another miracle to be accepted quickly as part of living in the city.

Sally and her parents were eventually to realize they were fated to challenge their city rather than quietly enjoy some of its advantages. There came a point in my observations of how they managed such a fate when I was puzzled at their continuing calm in the midst of danger. I frankly wondered . . . why they did not gather themselves together and leave. Sally's grandmother (during the worst of the ordeal, she had moved to be with her embattled children) gave the following explanation: "If we run away, we'll fool ourselves; you can't run away from being a colored man. It don't make any difference where you go—you has the same problem, one way or another." I asked her whether she thought those problems in any way comparable to those faced by white people— for example those few white families who were resisting the mob's will, defying its boycott to keep their children at school with Sally. "Yes," she replied firmly, "we is all the same under God, so we has the same problems; but colored folk has special ones, too. It's the same being colored as white, but it's different being colored, too." Then she repeated the words, nodding her agreement with them, "It's the same, but it's different."

·   ·   ·   ·   ·   ·   ·   ·   ·   ·   ·   ·   ·   ·   ·   ·   ·   ·

What interested me about the remarks of Sally's grandmother was that she gave me an essentially matter-of-fact explanation for her steadfastness: there was simply no alternative. A Negro cannot flee danger, try though he might. Danger is everywhere, a never ending consequence of his social and economic condition. Danger is written into history with his blood, into everyday customs by laws, into living itself by the size of his wages, the nature of his neighborhood. In contrast, every white parent I knew fell back upon another kind of reason for his actions. One father was a minister; he called upon his religious faith. Another parent was especially devoted to the education of her children; she could not stand idle while a school was destroyed, her children untaught. One family had only recently come to . . . [the city]; they did not "believe" in segregation—and they were stubborn and plucky enough to want to stand up for their beliefs, or, in this case, the absence of them.

·   ·   ·   ·   ·   ·   ·   ·   ·   ·   ·   ·   ·   ·   ·   ·   ·   ·

I do not think that situation . . . was unlike the general situation in our country, as it confronts Negro and white people. The stakes may usually be less grim, less distinctly defined, less dangerously at issue; but the Negro has his skin to help him establish the nature of his problems and his beliefs, while white people must grapple for other mainstays of self-awareness or faith. . . . I have come to see that children who grow up and experience the Negro's lot in our society—no matter how various its expressions—achieve at least some measure of self-definition. It may be insufficient, it may lead to ruin, yet it cannot be seen only as a burden. To quote again from Sally's grandmother: "We may not have anything, but at least we know why." . . .

What can be said about how Sally feels being a Negro, about how her grandmother feels, or any of the other children, the other adults I have met and come to know? All that has been said about the meaning of skin color to Negro children surely holds for Sally—and has always held for her parents and grandparents. Sally at six could tell me rather openly that she wished she were white. I have seen Negro children her age who denied and concealed similar wishes with great vehemence that they, in fact, had such wishes was all too clear from their drawings, games, and "innocent" or "unintended" remarks.

Still, as we grow, or live, we all want occasionally to be what we are not, or cannot really ever become. What must be done is to establish the relevance, the importance of Sally's fantasies about her skin for the rest of her life. To do so requires placing discrete psychological events (and the observations made by psychiatrists of those events) in the context of the general growth and development of the child, including, of course, the influences of society upon how he is reared and taught to regard himself.

For instance, fairly quickly after my encounter with Negro children I could see in drawing after drawing their sensitivity to the colors black and brown—and, conversely, to white, yellow, and orange. Their sketches revealed their sense of fear of white people, their sense of lack at not having white skin, their sense of foreboding at what the future held for them as Negroes. One child drew himself small and mutilated in contrast to white children; another pictured himself so noticeably larger and stronger that one had to wonder why. (When I did, I heard the following reply: "Well, you have to be big if you're not going to get killed.") Then there were children who never wanted to draw themselves or anyone else as Negro; or those who had no idea how to sketch their white classmates except by making them a lighter shade of brown.

Perhaps more interesting than such evidence of color-consciousness in children of five or six are the lessons associated with such awareness. Again and again when a Negro child wants to show in a drawing how crippled he may feel—or others may be—the arms he sketches suffer, while the legs seem quite intact, appropriately depicted, and often enough in motion. My wife first noticed this, and eventually mentioned it to one of the little Negro girls we knew best. She told us directly that "legs mean more than hands, so I gives them more attention. . . . If you can run, you're O. K., but if you take something you get in trouble." She smiled nervously and in embarrassment when I asked her what she had in mind "taking." She eventually told me that she had recently been punished for taking some candy from a dime-store counter. A saleslady had witnessed the deed, and strenuously reprimanded the girl and her mother. I discovered later that she had scolded the girl more for being Negro than an incipient thief. Since girls often want to steal at six, and many do, we must ask whether Negro children face special challenges in the course of learning the ordinary do's and don'ts of this world, let alone those special restrictions obviously associated with their position in our society.

My clinical impression—slowly consolidated over these past years of working with Negro children—is that most of the "usual" problems and struggles of growing up find an additional dimension in the racial context. In a very real sense being Negro serves to organize and render coherent many of the experiences, warnings, punishments, and prohibitions that Negro children face. The feelings of inferiority or worthlessness they acquire, the longing to be white they harbor and conceal, the anger at what they find to be their relatively confined and moneyless condition, these do not fully account for the range of emotions in many Negro children as they come to terms with the "meaning" of their skin color. Sally's grandmother said more concisely what I am struggling to say: "They can scream at our Sally, but she knows why, and she's not surprised. She knows that even when they stop screaming, she'll have whispers, and after them the stares. It'll be with her for life. . . . We tell our children that, so by the time they have children, they'll know how to prepare them. . . . It takes a lot of preparing before you can let a child loose in a white world. If you're black . . . it's like cloudy weather; you just don't see the sun much."

The "preparation" for such a climate of living begins in the first year of life. At birth the shade of the child's skin may be very important to his parents—so important that it determines in large measure how he is accepted, particularly in the many Negro marriages which bring together a range of genes which, when combined, offer the possibility of almost *any* color. What is often said about color-consciousness in Negroes . . . must be seen in its relentless effect upon the life of the mind, upon babies, and upon childrearing. A Negro sociologist . . . insisted to me that "when a Negro child is shown to his mother and father, the first thing they look at is his color, and then they check for fingers and toes." . . .

As infants become children, they begin to form some idea of how they look and how their appearance compares with that of others. They watch television, accompany their mothers to the local market or stores downtown. They play on the street and ride in cars which move through cities or small towns. They hear talk, at the table or in Sunday school, or from other children while playing. By the time they enter school, at five or six, to "begin" to learn, they have already learned some lessons of self-respect (or its absence) quite well. . . . Children . . . quickly learn to estimate who can vote, . . . who has the money to frequent this kind of restaurant or that kind of theater, . . . what groups of people contribute to our police force—and why. . . . They remark upon the scarcity of colored faces on television and I have heard them cheer the sight of a Negro on that screen. In the South they ask their parents why few if any policemen or bus drivers are colored. In the ghettos of the North they soon enough come to regard the Negro policeman or bus driver as specially privileged—as indeed he is, with his steady pay, with his uniform that calls for respect and signifies authority—and perhaps as an enemy in the inevitable clash. . . .

.   .   .   .

The Negro child growing up is . . . likely to be quite rigidly and fearfully certain about what he may do, where he may go, and who he eventually will be. In the desegregated schools of the South, where Southern whites have had a fresh opportunity and reason to watch Negro children closely, teachers have been especially impressed by what one of them called the "worldliness" of the colored child . . . referring to the shrewd, calculating awareness in children who have been taught—worried about, screamed at, slapped, and flogged in the process—the rules of the game as they apply to Negroes. [The teacher] . . . had come to realize that growing up as a Negro child had its special coherence and orderliness as well as its chaos. The children she was teaching were lonely, isolated, and afraid—a few of them in a large, only recently desegregated white elementary school . . . but they also knew exactly what they feared,

79

and exactly how to be as safe as possible in the face of what they feared.

For that matter, it is not simply that Negro children learn the bounds of their fate, the limits of the kinds of work allowed to them, the extent of their future disfranchisement, the confines of their social freedom, the edge of the residential elbowroom permitted them, the margin of free play, whim, or sport available to them now or within their grasp when they are grown. They learn how to make use of such knowledge, and in so doing gain quite gradually and informally an abiding, often tough sense of what is about them in the world, and what must be in them to survive. In the words of Sally's grandmother, "Sally can get through those mobs; she was born to, and one way or another she'll have to do it for the rest of her life."

So it is not all disorder and terror for these children. As they grow older, go to school, think of a life for themselves, they can envision a life which is quiet, pleasant, and uneventful for long stretches of time, or at least as much so as for any "other" children. That is, the Negro child will play and frolic, eat and sleep like all other children; and, though this may seem no great discovery, it is essential that it be mentioned in a discussion which necessarily singles out special pains or hazards for analysis. Sometimes when I read descriptions of "what it is like to be a Negro" I have to turn away in disbelief: the children I have been working with—in share-cropper cabins and migrant camps as well as in cities—simply do not resemble the ones portrayed. Perhaps it is impossible in any description to do justice to the continuity and contradiction of life, but we can at least try by qualifying our assumptions, by acknowledging that they do not encompass the entire range of human experience.

"It's like being two people: when I'm around here I'm just me; when I leave and go to school or go downtown, I'm just another person." A high school student . . . is speaking, a Negro youth who is trying to integrate those two facets of his personality as well as himself into a white school. Yet, not even his sharp, clear-cut statement can account for the range of sensibilities which develop in Negro children as a result of their race's history and present condition.

As in all matters of human behavior each Negro child or adult I have met has developed or is developing his or her own style of dealing with what is essentially a social experience that becomes for the individual a series of psychological ones capable of giving "significant" structure or form to a life. Some of the styles are well established in folklore and in the daily expectations of both whites and Negroes: subservience, calculated humiliation, sly ingratiation, self-mockery; or changing the tone somewhat, aloof indifference, suspicious withdrawal, sullen passivity, or grim, reluctant compliance. Again, in areas of diminished repression, where outright submission has been replaced by the possibility of social and racial disengagement or "co-existence," one sees impatience, or ill-tempered, measured distrust; indeed, in evidence is everything from irritability and barely concealed resentment to an almost numbing hatred and fury.

What most Negro children of ten or twelve have learned is a tendency, stimulated by the white man's presence or appearance, for one or (more likely) a mixture of several of these or other adaptive modes of dealing with him. The choice, of course, depends on the private life of the child, his general development of personality —there are reasons other than racial ones for being prone to good-humored supplication or to anger, despair, resignation, sulkiness, insensibility, or inertia. The manner of adjustment also varies, as I mentioned, by region and by class or occupation. . . .

.   .   , ...

If the white man must often deny his early, increasingly confusing friendliness with Negroes, the Negro has little choice but to come to terms with his early equally confusing awe, envy, and hate of whites, and his friendliness with them. "Keep your fear of the white man, I has to tell it to every child all the time until they knows it for themselves." I asked this poor, uneducated wife of a former sharecropper whether her children had only fear of whites. She shook her head. "They be jealous of them. Sometimes they might want to see how they live; so my husband drives them over and picks me up from work." (She worked as a maid in a comfortable . . . suburb, and her daughter was now at school with children who lived in that suburb.) "I told her, we can have all the rights they have, but you can't feel easy with them so fast. . . . I just make sure my kids know to be afraid."

The "ma'am" that the white child learns to drop the Negro child learns to say—say fearfully, say anxiously, say reluctantly, say eagerly, say out of habit, say with conviction, say and mean, or say with reservations that surely include a wide range of bitterness and resentment. Doubtless the experience of a Negro growing up

81

in . . . [a Northern city] is different from that of a Negro in the . . . [Deep South], but I think the common need persists everywhere in America for Negro youth to gauge their relationships to white people warily. While the white man loses part of his own life history, his own kindness or goodwill when he isolates his present self from his past feelings, the Negro loses part of his own life history, his natural self-protective assertiveness, his confidence with others and ease about himself, when he learns to separate his past experience of surprised indignation from his present sense of what the world expects and will demand. . . . One of the sit-in students we know best . . . is one of seven children, and the only one to show his kind of tough defiance of the laws and customs of his native . . . [state]. Why he? . . .

Listening to the taped interview (with him and his parents) once again, I saw that dreary row of houses on the unpaved street. . . . Though we were in the South, the December day was chilly; the house was drafty, and warmed by one of those gas burners that often enough explode. If you sit near them you sweat; if you move only a few feet away, the flame might as well be extinguished. I had asked why Lawrence was the one child in that home (his father is a frequently unemployed handyman, his mother a domestic) to take a stand against the . . . State Highway Patrol in order that he and others like him might register to vote.

"To tell the truth, I don't know," was the way his mother began her reply. Her husband was more equivocal: "I don't either, but I think it's because he's just stubborn, and he hasn't lost it like you do when you gets older." Now his mother's mind had been set in motion: "That's right. Lawrence always knew what he wanted, so he's just gone and stood up for it. Of course, I think all of us want the same thing he does. It's just in his nature to go after it more than others will." I wanted to know how that quality had taken root only in Lawrence, but they had no explanation. They did have some comments—and perhaps all the explanation there could be: "Lawrence does what he believes is right," his father said proudly, "but it's in the air these days for us to stand up and be counted. . . . Mind you, I'm not taking anything away from the boy, but I think all our children feel the same on being treated better. It's his age. The younger ones can't do anything because they're not yet grown; and the older ones, they've just had their dreams die." His wife took up that theme immediately: "You get older and get a family, and that's the end. But don't you think Lawrence is alone! Every colored child in America wants what he does. I'm his mother, and I'm proud of him; but I has to say the truth."

She clearly feared that what little distinction had come her family's way might dissolve in the face of a truth she had to acknowledge. Her husband . . . said what was to be the last word on the subject: "Anything Lawrence has done, we all want to do. He had a chance to do it, but all the kids were with him every inch. . . . I'll bet every colored boy in America has the same dream Lawrence has. Maybe only a few of them can do anything about it, but we all has the same dream." I think he is right; yet men have a number of dreams in them and some of them work at odds with others. Lawrence's determination—in the face of extreme danger—has simply not been matched by others, even those of his age. A common heritage and condition do not ensure either bravery or cowardice.

. . . A number of observers from several disciplines, have remarked upon the serious psychological problems facing large numbers of Negroes who live impoverished lives, in a social and cultural climate which commonly rejects them, and in families often enough unstable, disturbed, and split apart.

Of course, it is obvious that millions of Negroes survive such special strains—if not handily, then at least with no crippling mental disease. As a matter of fact, what is puzzling to those of us who have worked with the more penniless, "backward," rural Negroes is our continuing sense of the remarkable sturdiness and poise in many of them. Many others, of course, are tired, apathetic, almost lifeless; though even people in this latter group show a striking capacity to come alive when exposed to the momentum of social and political change.

.   .   .   .

In recent years I have found myself continually puzzled by the capacity of sharecroppers or migratory workers, the very poorest of our poor, and politically the most defenseless of our outcasts, to maintain for themselves and their children a striking quality of stubborn, willful endurance that is not only grim (I was expecting, even looking for that) but often enough resilient, light-hearted, and exceedingly canny. Now, to be droll, flexible, quick-witted, and sensible is to possess virtues presumably nourished in "civilized" societies. To be confronted with the degrading, humiliating poverty of Negro migrant farmers or sharecroppers is to wonder how humanity can even minimally maintain itself under such circumstances; the discovery of any refinements of mind or heart seems utterly surprising and unaccountable.

In the slums we can always—I think wrongly—fall back on our schools or general climate of city life to explain an alert, capable boy, or else summon those handy "genes." Conversely, the wide-spread violence and delinquency in the cities are attributed to the poor housing, the bad education, the joblessness in the ghettos. Among millions of Negroes in the South, still in rural or semi-rural situations, equivalent explanations do not hold. Many of the children are quite capable and impressive, with only dismal schools and few other "advantages" to be had; moreover, there are farming communities in the Black Belt which combine extreme hardship for Negroes with a relatively small incidence of crime among them. (Violence toward whites is out of the question, but in some of these areas there is little violence among Negroes, too.)

I find such observations unsettling. They lead us away from some of the prevalent "conclusions" of our time: that prejudice, segregation, and extreme poverty corrode the stamina of people and make them self-destructive or inert; that a move from the terror in . . . [the rural Deep South] to the earnest climate of progress in civil rights which characterizes many . . . cities is altogether desirable and beneficial for Negroes; that improving the lot of Negroes is an urgent problem lest millions of them succumb to, or perpetuate, the personal and public chaos that is so predominantly theirs.

.   .   .   .

. . . Alongside suffering I have encountered resilience and an incredible capacity for survival. To travel about with migrant workers, to stop with them as they visit their sharecropper brothers or cousins, is to realize how tenaciously and sternly they persist, as well as how unequipped they are for our white, middle-class world. Moreover, I will risk being called anything from a fool to a sentimental apologist for a dying order by insisting upon the fun, good times, and frolic I daily saw in these people. Of course, they have downcast and sour moments, too—often brought on by the presence of white people. Yet, as one man reminded me, "We can always forget them when they're gone, and most of the time they're just not here to bother us—we know they're always on our back, but it's when they get in front of us and try tripping us up that we get upset." I watched his angry petulance, his artful self-abasement with the white foreman on the farm he helped cultivate; I also saw how very pleasant and even sprightly he could be at home with his wife and children. "We has it rough, but we knows how to live with it, and we learned it so long ago it's second nature; so most of the time it's not so bad; tell the truth, it's only once in a while things get bad . . . so long as you keeps your wits and doesn't ask for but your rights." Even in segregated, impoverished rural areas there are "rights" in the sense that the social system is not erratic, chaotic, or inconsistent with its own (if peculiar and arbitrary) traditions.

. . . .

In general, I have been trying to indicate that I find the task of talking about "the Negro" difficult indeed, the more so because of how many individual Negro men, women, and children I know. Even their common suffering, a suffering that has cursed all Americans since the beginning of this country and has yet to be ended, fails to bind them together sufficiently to cause them to lose their individuality, a fact that may be sad for zealous social scientists but is ultimately hopeful for America.

There is, there must be, a certain danger in talking about millions of people as a group, whether we talk about their "negritude" or their chronicle of hurts and wants. Sometimes I feel I have gathered a mass of impressions about how Negroes, in contrast, say, to middle-class whites, live, think, and feel. Still the heart and soul of their existence, and the spirit which informs their lives, probably are as terribly various and stubbornly resistant to generalizations as those we call "ours."

I *do* know that there is a concrete *reality* in being an American Negro; that millions of people are tied down to it; that some of them are driven mad by it; that others are frightfully torn by its prospects; that the spectacle of what its consequences have been for this nation is not yet completed; that in its grip people have faltered, cowered, and pretended; that from its grip people have fled and battled their way; and that, finally, the worst and best in mankind have emerged.

Today any person or people is lucky to escape some kind of categorical approximation. The Negro, surely, has not suffered alone on *that* account. Nor has his meaning for white people been left uncatalogued. I hear talk about his childlike behavior in the face of a culture that so regards him. I hear that he is a symbol of this or that to nervous, sexually troubled whites; or that he is himself foolishly, childishly wanton and bold, or fearfully thwarted and stunted. I hear that he has his special black soul, mysterious and wonderful, defying description—the very attempt to describe it being a characteristic of the white soul.

Who can limit by any list of attributes the nature of any person, the possibilities in any group of people? We cannot forsake our informed attempts to do just that, particularly in the case of those kept so long outside us while so deeply and sacrificially within us. I would only hope that some day soon the Negro will achieve an order of freedom that will make our descriptions and categories no longer so relevant—indeed, not only out of date, but out of order. . . . The dignity of the Negro is not served *either* by seeing only his exploitation or by turning his condition into yet another excuse for fake envy, based on romanticized celebrations of what in point of fact was disastrous suffering. A Negro girl . . . told me once: "Some ways it's not bad at all, but other ways it's worse than anything can be." The point is that people can be frightfully damaged; yet their lives unfold in a promising fashion, so that they are ready for such actual promises as the present civil rights movement hopes to realize. . . . The Negro's struggle for his life and limb, for his rights, for his own worth and excellence, reminds any of us who care to be reminded that all of us share this struggle and will always need one another's example and help in coming to terms with it. . . .

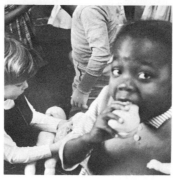

Is desegregation of faculty educationally sound?

Elimination of time and space as factors in travel and communication are increasing the amount of interaction that Americans have and will have with other peoples around the world. Three-fourths of those people are nonwhite. Therefore, children of both races who are now in school will have increasing need for positive attitudes toward the opposite race. When white children have Negro teachers, and Negro children have white teachers, respect for and acceptance of each other will develop and racial difference will cease to be a valid reason for rejection.

Civil rights legislation is resulting in increasing numbers of whites who work side by side with Negroes and as employers and employees of Negroes. This again requires positive interracial attitudes which will be fostered when teachers of both races work together and when their pupils benefit from changes in attitudes that come from satisfying interpersonal relations among faculty members.

The schools are now in a position of leadership in the nation. Race relations, which is a crucial national problem, must be discussed in school. An integrated faculty will become an example of how good interpersonal race relations can be. This gives promise of good group relations across race lines.

Children need role models. Negro children in desegregated schools need Negro teachers whose values and behavior patterns they can learn and with whom they can communicate thoughts and emotions which they cannot yet tell white teachers about. The nation needs to create a new image of the Negro in order to break down the stereotype. Negro teachers provide examples of Negroes who are middle class, educated, and successful in a high status profession.

Negro teachers whose jobs have disappeared when children were transferred have the right to positions in desegregated schools. If even one is deprived of that right on the basis of race alone, the rights of all teachers are jeopardized.

What a racially integrated classroom is like

Desegregation in education is not new. For at least fifty years, Negro and white pupils have sat together in the secondary schools of every Northern city that has Negro citizens. In many of those cities, some of the Negro children also went to elementary schools in which at least some classmates were white. Were any of the classrooms in those schools integrated? Did anyone ever bother to find out?

In the fight to eliminate persistent discriminatory college admission quotas, race was eliminated from school records. When questioned about the nature of the school population, it became customary for school superintendents to answer, "I don't know how many Negroes we have. We keep no records of race." However, in an effort to better intergroup relations, both racial and religious, school projects on "brotherhood" or "living together" became popular.

There is little doubt that studies of school records, were race inserted in them, would show that more Negro children were away more often; that their achievement scores were lower; that they were frequently punished; that more were over age because they were kept back more frequently; that their parents were hard to reach, they wouldn't come to PTA; that they took part in few if any after-school activities; and that more of them left school as soon as the law allowed—fewer were graduated from high schools and few got into college preparatory courses. Educators did seek the reasons why, but many school people were content to leave it at that, believing in the depths of their minds that race was the cause.

In spite of segregation and inequality of education, individual Negro students did lift their heads and got recognition. Sports and music were the first areas opened to them, and many excelled in those fields as the result of ability, plus hard work. But many teachers called them "the exception that proved the rule" and fitted them into the stereotype which characterizes Negroes as powerful and musical—"they have rhythm and strong bodies."

But there were and are teachers and administrators who care what happens to every child. In their schools, integration comes to be a way of life. What does that way look like?

Children are not segregated by ability, Negroes at the bottom. In the classroom, they sit (as others do) where they can do the best work. The prestige classes such as Latin, French, algebra, and physics have Negro pupils. Negroes hold some of the top student offices—even the presidency—having been elected on the basis of their qualifications. Negroes are members of prestige (as well as ordinary) clubs such as ballet, journalism, bowling, dramatics, and experimental science. Student hosts for the day and building guides and messengers include both races.

When integration is a fact in school life, in the primary rooms Negro children are in the top as well as the middle and slow reading groups. In upper-elementary and secondary rooms, Negroes are among the committee leaders and secretaries. They also do their share, but no more, of the housekeeping chores. And the distribution of children and work is all done naturally, without self-consciousness or noticeable effort. Teachers pay attention to clues which indicate prejudice, rejection, and exclusion on the basis of race and take whatever corrective measures are required.

In the integrated classroom, Negro and white children sit next to each other, share their work, ask each other for help, and get it. They have equal opportunity to answer questions, to put their work on the board, and to display their talents and abilities. Race does not figure in the teacher's or pupils' minds when recognition, praise, and rewards are distributed.

Name-calling and scapegoating are not practiced in integrated classrooms; neither do children fight with each other. However, children of both races do not hesitate to remind each other of the limits of behavior they and their teachers set up together.

In integrated classrooms, teachers do not have pets of either race. Their watchwords are impartiality and equality of opportunity to learn. This does not mean that all children are given the same work to do, in the same way, at the same time, from the same books. Quite the contrary. There is less and less mass instruction, more pupil-teacher planning, more sharing of responsibilities through committee or small group work, and the use of vicarious and direct learning experiences as well as printed materials on a wide range of reading levels.

In the integrated room, children are not compared on the basis of worth and are not pitted against each other in merciless competition. They are not compared to the shame and humiliation of those of both races who think, talk, and learn more slowly. Groups and individuals evaluate their processes and products and their performance as leaders and followers. Teachers evaluate rather than mark each child's work, encouraging each to do better than he did before.

The teachers of integrated classes never indulge in breaking children down, "putting them in their place," or using other methods of insulting white, Negro, or any other minority group child. Race is not a target for derision or pity. Negroes are not looked down upon or exalted; they are neither mascots nor scapegoats for teacher or classmates.

Nonwhite and all ethnic groups, as well as white children and teachers, respect each other when integration exists, and at least some of them become friends across group lines. However, the climate is such that everyone can express his feelings without fear of reprisal; this is not a goody-goody place in which hypocrisy may be developed.

In the truly integrated classroom, high-quality teaching and learning go on but the room will not be silent all the time nor will children always sit quietly in rows of desks or chairs. Uniformity and regimentation are not required. There is also time for fun and laughter. Teacher and students are relaxed and at times seem to be not quite on best behavior, but group and personal controls have emerged and any necessary punishments for infractions are administered without personal bias.

The integrated classroom is one in which children are learning the Judeo-Christian and democratic values. They know the principles of democracy and are developing the skills they need to practice the democratic processes. Each places high value on and accepts other individuals on the basis of personal worth without regard for differences of race, religion, ethnic origin, social class, or ability. Each pupil is finding his own identity and making peace with himself and others as he prepares for abundant, generous, effective living in our democratic and multi-ethnic world.

The challenge to teachers is clear. The promise to students is fulfillment of the American dream.

SELECTED REFERENCES

Books

Allport, Gordon. *The Nature of Prejudice*. Boston: Beacon Press, 1954.
Discussion of the legal, social, and economic aspects of group prejudice, with special emphasis on the deeper psychological causes of hatred and conflict.

Bloom, Benjamin; Davis, Allison; and Hess, Povert. *Compensatory Education for Cultural Deprivation*. New York: Holt, Rinehart, 1965.
Contains good recommendations for innovations and an excellent annotated bibliography.

Clark, Kenneth B. *Dark Ghetto: Dilemma of Social Power*. New York: Harper and Row, 1965.
A documentation of the myriad ways in which society cheats Negroes. It examines the ghetto in terms of the social dynamics, the psychology, the pathology, the schools, and the power structure, and suggests strategy for change.

Combs, Arthur W., ed. *Perceiving, Behaving, Becoming. A New Focus for Education*. Washington, D.C.: Association for Supervision and Curriculum Development, 1961. $4.50.
Describes how schools may help to develop fully functioning and self-actualizing persons.

Goodman, Mary Ellen. *Race Awareness in Young Children*. New York: Collier Books, 1964.
A study of nursery school children, what they think and feel about race and how they learned it. Refutes the idea that young children do not have prejudice.

Grossack, Martin M. *Mental Health and Segregation*. New York: Springer Publishing Co., 1963.
Covers the major dimensions of mental health and segregation: problems of morale; studies of children, adolescents, adults; approaches to mental health; and contains an extensive bibliography.

Kvaraceus, William, and others. *Negro Self-Concept: Implications for School and Citizenship*. New York: McGraw-Hill Book Co., 1965.
Report of the conference on "The Relationship of Education to Self-Concept in Negro Children and Youth." Examines forces that create negative self-concepts in Negro children. Identifies and delineates the school's role in helping to create a more positive self-image.

Noar, Gertrude. *Teaching and Learning the Democratic Way*. Englewood Cliffs, N.J.: Prentice Hall, 1963.
Based upon actual classroom experience in which an interdisciplinary approach and pupil-teacher planning are used to develop units on intergroup relations. The values and principles of democracy and the democratic processes are learned through practice in using them.

Pettigrew, Thomas F. *Profile of the Negro American*. Princeton, N.J.: Van Nostrand, 1964.
A survey and interpretation of research on Negro American intelligence

and other psychological factors. Organized into three main sections: American Negro Personality, Racial Differences, and the American Negro Protest.

Rockwell,_____, and Liddle,_____. *Modifying the School Experience of Culturally Handicapped Children in Primary Grades.* Quincy, Ill.: Youth Development Commission, 1964.
Gathered from action research projects, the contents are of special importance to elementary teachers in center-city schools.

Rose, Peter. *They and We: Racial and Ethnic Relations in the U.S.* New York: Random House, 1964.
A synopsis of some of the principal aspects of minority group relations in the United States.

Taba, Hilda, and others. *Diagnosing Human Relations Needs.* Washington, D.C.: American Council on Education, 1951. 155 pp.
Deals with discovering children's needs through methods such as role playing, open-end questions, and the deep interview.

Trager, Helen G., and Yarrow, Marian Radke. *They Learn What They Live: A Study of Prejudice in Young Children.* New York: Harper and Brothers, 1952.
An action research project in Philadelphia, done in connection with in-service education programs, interpreted and evaluated the genesis and growth of prejudice in first- and second-grade children.

Pamphlets

Beaucham, Mary; Ardelle, Llewellyn; and Worley, Vivienne S. *Building Brotherhood: What Can Elementary Schools Do?* New York: National Conference of Christians and Jews, n.d. 78 pp.

Crosby, Muriel, ed. *Reading Ladders for Human Relations.* Fourth edition. Washington, D.C.: American Council on Education, 1963.
Bibliography of books on family life, growing up, belonging to groups, socioeconomic differences, and adjusting to new situations.

Deutsch, Martin, and others. *Guidelines for Testing Minority Children.* New York: Anti-Defamation League of B'nai B'rith, 1964. 18 pp.
Discussion of why IQ tests are not valid measures of intelligence in most children.

Fairfax County Schools, Department of Instruction. *A Guide to Intergroup Education.* Fairfax, Va.: Fairfax County School Board, 1965. 56 pp.

Gnadey, William J. *Controlling Classroom Misbehavior.* What Research Says to the Teacher, No. 32. Prepared by the American Educational Research Association in cooperation with the Department of Classroom Teachers. Washington, D.C.: National Education Association, December 1965. 31 pp.

Grambs, Jean D. *Understanding Intergroup Relations.* What Research Says to the Teacher, No. 21. Prepared by the American Educational Research Association in cooperation with the Department of Classroom Teachers. Washington, D.C.: National Education Association, Revised edition, 1965. 31 pp.

Heaton, Margaret M. *Feelings Are Facts.* New York: National Conference of Christians and Jews. 1964.

McWhirter, Mary Esther. *Books for Friendship.* Philadelphia: American Friends Service Committee, 1962. 64 pp.
Annotated list of 500 books, graded from kindergarten to upper junior high school, which attempts to "depict fairly, accurately, and sympa-

thetically people of all religious, racial, regional, national, and economic groups."

Montagu, Ashley. *What We Know About Race*. New York: Anti-Defamation League of B'nai B'rith, 1965. 40 pp. (plus teacher's guide).
Can be used as the center around which to plan a unit in secondary schools.

National Education Association and American Association of School Administrators, Educational Policies Commission. *Education and the Disadvantaged American*. Washington, D.C.: the Commission, 1962. 39 pp.

National Education Association, Department of Elementary-Kindergarten-Nursery Education. *Prevention of Failure*. Washington, D.C.: the Department, 1965. 95 pp.

New York State Education Department. *Intergroup Relations: A Resource Handbook for Elementary School Teachers Grades 4, 5, and 6*. Albany: the Department, 1964. 48 pp.

———. *Intergroup Relations: A Resource Handbook for 12th Grade Social Studies*. Albany: the Department, 1965. 56 pp.

Noar, Gertrude. *Information Is Not Enough*. New York: Anti-Defamation League of B'nai B'rith, 1961. 26 pp.
An overall view of the need for intergroup relations in education.

———. *Living with Difference*. New York: Anti-Defamation League of B'nai B'rith, 1965. 15 pp.
Discusses and illustrates the positive value of human differences in all aspects of human life.

Pennsylvania State Committee on Human Relations. *Our Greatest Challenge: Human Relations*. Harrisburg: Pennsylvania State Department of Public Instruction, 1962. 56 pp.
Directions to teachers at all grade levels for content and methods of teaching human relations.

Redl, Fritz; Sheviakow, George V.; and Richardson, Sybil K. *Discipline*. Washington, D.C.: Association for Supervision and Curriculum Development, 1965. 64 pp.

Tumin, Melvin M., ed. *Race and Intelligence: A Scientific Evaluation*. New York: Anti-Defamation League of B'nai B'rith, 1963. 56 pp.
Refutes the myth of racial inferiority.

United Nations. *Teaching Human Rights: A Handbook for Teachers*. New York: Office of Public Information, 1963. 79 pp.

Van Til, William. *Prejudiced—How Do People Get That Way?* New York: Anti-Defamation League of B'nai B'rith, 1957. 32 pp. (plus teacher's supplement).
Can be used as the center around which to plan a unit in secondary school.

Young, Margaret B. *How To Bring Up Your Children Without Prejudice*. New York: Public Affairs Pamphlets, 1965. 20 pp.

Special Materials on Negro Americans

History of Negroes. Eight filmstrips. New York: McGraw-Hill Book Co.

Hughes, Langston, and Meltzer, Milton. *A Pictorial History of the Negro in America*. New York: Crown, 1962.
Names and events important in the Negro past are given, from the first slave ships to the present. The simple text makes this a useful reference.

More noteworthy are the 1,000 illustrations—prints, engravings, and photographs.

Leading American Negroes. Six filmstrips, with records and teacher's manual. Chicago: Society for Visual Education (1345 West Diversey).

"Negro Americans." New York: Time Magazine. (Reprint from January 3, 1964, issue.)
Contains pictures and short biographies of Negroes in various phases of American life. Also has an extensive bibliography of books written about the Negro in the United States.

Portraits of outstanding Negroes. New York: Friendship Press.

Periodicals

American Education. Washington, D.C.: U.S. Office of Education.

Journal of Negro Education. Washington, D.C.: Howard University Press.

Southern Education Report. Nashville, Tenn.: Southern Education Reporting Service.

Sources of Information

American Civil Liberties Union, 170 Fifth Avenue, New York, N.Y.

American Friends Service Committee, 160 North 15th Street, Philadelphia, Pa. 19107

American Jewish Committee, 165 East 56th Street, New York, N.Y. 10022

Anti-Defamation League of B'nai B'rith (ADL), 315 Lexington Avenue, New York, N.Y. 10016

National Association for the Advancement of Colored People (NAACP), 20 West 40th Street, New York, N.Y. 10018

National Conference of Christians and Jews (NCCJ), 43 West 57th Street, New York, N.Y. 10019

National Urban League, 14 East 48th Street, New York, N.Y.

Southern Regional Council, 5 Forsyth Street, N.W., Atlanta, Ga. 30303

U.S. Department of the Interior, Bureau of Indian Affairs, Washington, D.C.

Gertrude Noar

Miss Gertrude Noar has drawn upon her rich and varied experiences in the writing of this book. She has been an elementary and secondary school teacher, a high school principal, a university professor, a consultant to schools and teachers throughout the country, and has long devoted her energy and skills to improving human relations and working for human rights, with special reference to the education of children. For fifteen years Miss Noar was the national director of education for the Anti-Defamation League of B'nai B'rith. She now serves as a consultant to the Subcommittee on the Human Rights of Educators of the NEA Commission on Professional Rights and Responsibilities.

In addition to directing institutes and workshops for teachers and lay groups, Miss Noar has written several books and numerous pamphlets and articles. Among her most recent contributions are *Living With Difference* (Anti-Defamation League, 1965) and *Teaching and Learning the Democratic Way* (Prentice Hall, 1963).

A native of Philadelphia, Miss Noar received her bachelor's and master's degrees from the University of Pennsylvania, with concentrations in education, psychology, and sociology. She continued her graduate study at Columbia University, the University of Chicago, Pennsylvania State University, and Oxford University in England.

And you America
Cast you the real reckoning for your present?
The lights and shadows of your future, good or evil?
To girlhood, boyhood look, the teacher and the school.

Walt Whitman
"Leaves of Grass"

Book design by
Brooke Todd and Associates

Photographs by
Joseph Di Dio
Chief, Photo Section
NEA Division of Publications
and
Carl Purcell